人生を豊かに生きるために必要なものは何か
理想の高齢者施設を求めて
――ジュドソン・リタイアメント・コミュニティに学ぶ――

梶村慎吾　編・著

What do we need to live our lives with satisfaction?
To make ideal facilities for the elderly
—learning from Judson Retirement Community—

Edited by Kajimura Shingo

目次

Contents

Part One
What do we need to live our lives with satisfaction?

1. To live our lives with satisfaction 10
(1) The principle is for the residents   10
(2) Retirement Community   14
(3) The Eden Alternative   16
(4) To introduce Judson to Japanese people   20
(5) CIP (Council of International Programs)   22
2. CIP chose Judson for me to study as an intern 24
(1) Participate in the CIP program   24
(2) Departure   26
(3) Judson is in Cleveland   30
(4) Judson Manor   32
3. Working together 34
(1) To study many fields of works   34
(2) Difference between the two countries   36
4. Task of Social Work Department 40
(1) About the fee   40
(2) When they get weaker   44
5. Reminiscence Hour 46
(1) Reminiscence as psychotherapy   46
(2) Reminiscence hour on another day   50
6. At Day Enrichment Center 54
(1) The activity   54
(2) The program   54
7. From the Chief Financial Officer 60
8. Subject of Management 64

第1部
人生を豊かに生きるために必要なものは何か
1 人生を豊かに生きるために ……………………………… 11
(1) 利用者本位 11
(2) 退職者コミュニティ 15
(3) エデン・オールターナティブ 17
(4) ジュドソンの紹介をしたい 21
(5) CIP（カウンシル・オブ・インターナショナル・プログラムズ） 23
2 CIPは私の研修先としてジュドソンを選んでくれた ……………… 25
(1) CIP研修への参加 25
(2) 出発 27
(3) ジュドソンはクリーブランドにある 31
(4) ジュドソンメナー 33
3 共に働く ……………………………………………………… 35
(1) 多くの部署の働きを学ぶ 35
(2) 日本とのちがい 37
4 ソーシャルワークの課題 ………………………………… 41
(1) 費用負担について 41
(2) 体力が弱ってきたとき 45
5 回想法の時間 ……………………………………………… 47
(1) 心理療法としての回想法 47
(2) 別の日の回想法の時間 51
6 デイサービスセンターにて ……………………………… 55
(1) 活動 55
(2) ある日のプログラム 55
7 最高財務責任者に聞く …………………………………… 61
8 経営管理上の考慮 ………………………………………… 65

Part Two
Judson at University Circle 1906–2006 A Century of Excellence
1. Preface 72
2. Introduction 76
3. It was Cleveland's Gilded Age... 78
4. Community Partner and Resource 92
5. The Heart and Soul 100
6. Leading with Compassion and Vision 116
7. Creating a Legacy 122
8. Building on Success 124
9. Epilogue 128

Part Three
Council of International Programs USA (CIPUSA)
1. The interview to Dr. Ollendorff tells us about the birth of CIP 132
2. The wish of Dr. Ollendorff and CIPUSA 142
3. Council of International Fellowship (CIF) 144

Source books and Reference material 148
Postscript 150

Photography: Getty Images, The Judson Archives, Bill Pappas Photography, Alejandro Rivera Photography, Taxel Image Group, Karen Ollis Toula of Crescent Moon Art, University Circle Incorporated Archives, The Western Reserve Historical Society Archives and Judson residents' family photos.

第2部
ユニバーシティサークルにおけるジュドソン 1906—2006 卓越の一世紀
1 はしがき ……………………………………………………… 73
2 前置き ………………………………………………………… 77
3 それはクリーブランドの金色に輝く時代 …………………… 79
4 コミュニティパートナーと地域の資源としてのジュドソン… 93
5 心と魂 ………………………………………………………… 101
6 共感とビジョンをもって先頭に立つ ………………………… 117
7 次代に残すべきもの ………………………………………… 123
8 建設計画の成功の上に ……………………………………… 125
9 エピローグ …………………………………………………… 129

第3部
カウンシル・オブ・インターナショナル・プログラムズ USA (CIPUSA)
1 オレンドルフ博士へのインタビューが伝える CIP 誕生の物語 …… 133
2 オレンドルフ博士の願いと CIPUSA ………………………… 143
3 カウンシル・オブ・インターナショナル・フェロウシップ (CIF) …… 145

出典・引用参考文献 …………………………………………… 149
あとがき ………………………………………………………… 151

第 1 部

人生を豊かに生きるために必要なものは何か

Part One

What do we need to live our lives with satisfaction?

Part One: What do we need to live our lives with satisfaction?

1. To live our lives with satisfaction

(1) The principle is for the residents

What is the important factor to live our lives with satisfaction in our latter half of lives?
In 1996 and 1997, I experienced and studied as an intern at Judson Retirement Community in Cleveland, Ohio, USA. It is a not-for-profit organization. At that time I was an administrator of a facility of social welfare for the elderly.

Judson had two big facilities Judson Park and Judson Manor. The residents numbered about 450, the adult day care participants were about 30 and the health & wellness members (not living at Judson) were about 200. The employees were about 500.
Since then the number of health & wellness members has increased. Over 500 youngsters monthly come to Judson through the growing network of community collaborations including the curriculum-driven partnership with local schools now.

In ordinary case those who want to be residents of Judson come to Judson when they are healthy and active. They enjoy their lives as they like. Some residents study at the neighboring university by auditing classes. Some are working as volunteers at Judson or in the neighboring communities.
A resident had organized a hand-bell music group at Judson and had served as its conductor. She was about 90 years old, gathering the autobiographies of several tens of the residents. She had been practicing to handle a personal computer and

1 人生を豊かに生きるために

(1) 利用者本位

　長寿社会にあって高齢者が満足感を持って後半の人生を生きるために必要な条件とは何か。

　1996年から97年にかけて、当時高齢者福祉施設の管理者を務めていた私は、縁あって4か月間、アメリカ・オハイオ州クリーブランドにあるジュドソン・リタイアメント・コミュニティという非営利の退職者のための総合高齢者施設で研修をする機会があった。

　当時2つの大きな施設を持ち、施設に居住する利用者約450人、デイサービス利用者約30人、地域からの健康プログラム参加者約200人、職員約500人という規模であった。

　その後地域からの健康プログラムへの参加者は大幅に増加しており、また現在では地域の学校のカリキュラムに組み入れられた相互協力関係を含む地域社会とのネットワークにより、毎月500人以上の若者がジュドソンを訪れている。

　通常、ジュドソンには高齢者が元気なうちに入居し、自分の好きな生き方を自由に楽しむ。

　ある人は近くにある大学で聴講生となって勉強している。ある人はボランティア活動を施設内や地域社会で行っている。ある人は施設内のハンドベルグループを組織し、その指揮をしている。

　その人は90歳に近いが、施設の入居利用者（通所のデイサービス利用者と区別して、以下ではレジデントという）何十人かの自分史を聞き書きしてまとめており、パソコンの練習をしている。また施設内で子供たちにピアノを教えていたこともあった。

　利用者同士の交流も自由であり盛んである。施設内で結婚する人もいる。

　ジュドソンパークとジュドソンメナーという2施設があるが、そ

Part One: What do we need to live our lives with satisfaction?

had taught children to play the piano at Judson.
Residents go about with others freely. There were some residents who had gotten married at Judson. There is a resident council and a resident association in the two facilities (Judson Park and Judson Manor) which can decide the common matters of their daily lives. The president and chairperson of the council and the association are the members of the Board of Directors of the Judson Services, Inc..(*)
Judson calls the way of life there "Smart Living".

Judson is a not-for-profit organization and moreover, the representatives of the residents are the members of the board of directors of it, so that it is guaranteed that the principle of the management is for the residents.

The residents can move to assisted living when they come to need assistance for living. And they can also move to a special Alzheimer center if they need. The staff is very conscious not to let them feel depressed when they have to move.

(*)
There are 4 residents on the Board of Directors. Two are elected members with voting rights. One is from Judson Park and one is from Judson Manor. These two residents serve on the Judson Services, Inc. Board Marketing Committee.
The other two are the current Judson Park Resident Council President and the current Judson Manor Resident Association Chairperson. These two do not have voting rights. They also serve on the Judson Services, Inc. Board Finance Committee as non-voting members.

のそれぞれにレジデントの組織があり、生活についての共通事項を決定できる自治組織の性格を持つ。代表者は施設経営団体の理事会の一員となっている。※

　施設ではこのような生き方を「スマートリビング（スマートな生き方、又はかしこい生き方）」と呼んでいる。

　非営利組織であるうえにレジデント代表が理事会メンバーなので、利用者本位の経営が行われることが保証されている。
　加齢により体力が落ちてくると要支援棟へ移動することができ、さらにたとえアルツハイマー病になっても施設の別棟で生活できる。職員はその際、特にレジデントが暗い気持にならない配慮の重要性を自覚し実践している。

※法人の理事会メンバーにレジデントから４名が加わっている。２名は選出された理事で投票権を持つ。１人はジュドソンパークから、他の１人はジュドソンメナーから出ている。この２人の理事は、法人 Judson Services, Inc. の理事会のマーケティング委員会のメンバーである。他の２名は２つの施設の自治組織と言っていいレジデント委員会のそれぞれ現在の会長で、投票権を持たない。彼らはまた法人理事会の財務委員会の投票権のないメンバーとなっている。

(2) Retirement Community

Retirement Communities belong to "Yuryo (charged)" facilities for the elderly in Japan.
The American social security system is different from the Japanese system. In Japan we have the public long term care insurance system for people from 40 years old, and the public health insurance system for all people.
In America they have medicare for the elderly and medicaid for those who need public assistance. They have to pay the fee at their own expense or by private insurance to receive various services such as medical treatment, day care, skilled nursing and so on unless they can use these public social security systems.

When someone wants to be a resident of Judson, it must be confirmed that he or she can pay the fee through life.
But if he or she unfortunately can't pay the fee for some reason halfway, Judson pays.
Judson has the Judson Foundation under the parent company, Judson Services, Inc. The foundation purpose is for fund raising.
Judson uses a part of the raised funds for the residents who need monetary supports. Therefore, no residents have to leave Judson against their will.
Formerly a department of the parent organization was in charge of fund raising.

Judson wishes to make the community as follows.
Residents live as they want, keep the high level of quality of life as they wish and live in good relation with one another

(2) 退職者コミュニティ

　この退職者コミュニティといわれる種別の施設は日本でいえば有料高齢者施設（有料老人ホーム）に属する。
　アメリカの社会保障制度は40歳以上の国民を対象とする介護保険や全国民を対象とする健康保険制度のある日本とは異なっており、アメリカの高齢者医療保険制度メディケアや低所得者に対する医療扶助制度メディケイド等公的制度を利用できる場合以外には、医療・デイケア・デイサービスや寝たきり高齢者への入所サービス等の費用を自己負担や私的保険で賄わなければならない。

　入所契約締結の際に一生費用負担ができることを確認して入所が決められるが、不幸にして何らかの事情で途中で負担できなくなった人については、親組織Judson Services, Inc.の下に募金部門というべき傘下の組織としてJudson Foundation（ジュドソン財団）があり、その組織に寄せられた寄金の一部は費用負担ができなくなった人のための補助に使われている。そのため途中で退去しなければならなくなる人はいない。かつては親組織の募金部門であったものが現在では別組織として分離されたものである。

　ジュドソンはレジデントができる限り自分の生きたいように生き、自らの望むように質の高い生活を続けることができ、さらにレジデント相互にまた地域社会と良い関係を持てる共同体としての施設を目指している。私が滞在している間にも近隣の子供たちから施設のレジデントへペンフレンドになってほしいという内容の手紙が来ていた。近隣コミュニティとのつながりが強い。
　体力や健康が衰えてくると、それぞれの体力に応じた無理のない生活環境を用意し、支援やケアを行う。施設では、ここでレジデントが自分らしい充実感のある生き方ができる「スマートリビング」が実現できることを目指しており、身体運動を行うこと、知的刺激を高めること、社会と密接に関わることをそのための重要な要素と

and with the neighboring communities.

When I stayed at Judson, children in the neighborhood sent a letter to the residents to ask them to be their pen-friends.

Judson has close contact with the neighboring communities.

When the residents get weaker, Judson prepares a suitable living environment for them, and assists or cares for them as much as needed.

Judson focuses its efforts on preparing the condition for "smart living" that the residents can feel enrichment and fulfillment of their lives.

The key components for smart living are physical activity, encouraging intellectual stimulation and close contact with the community. Through wellness programs and so on, the residents have close contacts with people in the neighboring communities. .

The people in the neighboring communities welcome the close relation with Judson for enrichment of their lives, too.

This "Judson's way" suggests to us, beyond the borders of countries and cultures, what we need to live happily and to the fullest, and what is wished for in the facilities for the elderly.

(3) The Eden Alternative

I have kept in touch with Judson at least once a year. I received the centennial publication of Judson in 2006. The title was "Judson at University Circle 1906-2006, A Century of Excellence". In it, it was reported that Judson had stepped into a new stage to embrace the Eden Alternative. The Eden

して支援していく。

　健康プログラムを中心として、レジデントが地域の人々との交流を図り、地域の人々とのつながりを深めていく。そのことが地域の人々にとっても人生を豊かにするものとして歓迎される。

　このようなジュドソンの在り方は、人が幸せを感じ、生きがいのある人生を歩むために何が必要か、また高齢者施設に求められるものは何かについて、国境や文化を超えて多くの示唆をわれわれに与えてくれると感じた。

(3) エデン・オールターナティブ

　ジュドソンと私との間には毎年手紙のやり取りがあったが、2006年の創立100周年記念誌が私の手元に送られてきた。「ユニバーシティサークルにおけるジュドソン 1906－2006 卓越の一世紀」というタイトルであった。その中で、1999年にジュドソンは「エデン・オールターナティブ（エデンの園に代わるものの意味）」という非営利

Part One: What do we need to live our lives with satisfaction?

Alternative is a not-for profit organization.

The philosophy of it is as follows (from the Home page of the Eden Alternative, 30 June 2008):
The Eden Alternative has the belief that aging should be a continued stage of development and growth, rather than a period of decline, and that facilities for the elderly must be where the residents lead lives worth living.
It intends to transform the facilities for the elderly into the larger community of both elders and their care partners living out of the facilities. The facilities which have adopted this belief typically are filled with plants and animals, and at the same time are regularly visited by children.
The head office of this organization is in Texas, USA.
It has over 300 registered homes in the US, Canada, Europe and Australia.

When I read it, I thought that its idea was originally on the same root and basis with Judson. I felt it was quite natural that Judson embraced the Eden Alternative and fashioned its "brand of Eden".
When I was at Judson as an intern, Judson had been chosen as one of the 20 best Continuing Care Retirement Communities in America by "New Choices' Magazine" of the "Readers Digest's" publication.

Judson has been further refining its distinguished characteristics.

団体の主唱する運営方針を取り込み、新しい段階に入っていることを伝えていた。

　この団体の主唱する考えは、おおよそ次のとおりである（同団体のホームページ2008.6.30より）。
　歳を重ねることは、衰えていく過程ではなく、発展と成長の継続するステージであるべきだとの信念のもとに、高齢者施設は生きがいのある人生を過ごせる場でなければならないと考える。
　施設に生活する高齢者と施設外に住むケアパートナーとのより大きな共同体に施設を変えていこうというものである。この信念を取り入れた施設の典型は、緑の自然に囲まれ、生き物とのふれあいがあり、子供たちが定期的に訪れてくるようなホームである。
　この団体の本部はアメリカ・テキサス州にあり、この運動に参加している施設・団体はアメリカ・カナダ・ヨーロッパ・オーストラリアに合計300以上ある。

　これを読んだとき、それはもともとジュドソンの考えと方向を同じくするものであり、ジュドソンがこの運動のグループに加わり、独自のエデンブランドを創り上げたと書かれていることを自然の成り行きと感じた。
　私が研修のため訪れた当時、ジュドソンはリーダーズダイジェスト社の雑誌「ニューチョイスイズマガジン」によって全米で20の最優秀継続的ケア退職者コミュニティの1つに選ばれていた。現在、ジュドソンの特色にさらに磨きがかかってきているようである。

Part One: What do we need to live our lives with satisfaction?

(4) To introduce Judson to Japanese people

In July, 2007, I attended the 27th Council of International Fellowship (CIF) Conference in Cleveland, commemorating the 50th Anniversary of Council of International Programs USA (CIPUSA) that invited me to the CIP program in 1996 and 1997. Through the program I studied as an intern at Judson. CIF is the organization of the past participants in CIP programs from various countries.

I wanted to see the people again who I had met in 1996 and 1997.
I visited Judson to see Ms. Cynthia Dunn, President & CEO to express my hearty thanks for offering me the wonderful experiences as an intern. I told her my idea to introduce Judson to Japanese people. Fortunately I got her reply to cooperate on my plan.

In the centennial publication of Judson in 2006, the history and the works of Judson are written. The principle and philosophy of Judson that sustain the high level services are shown. It contains the wisdom to live a happy life with satisfaction in the latter part of life, and a lot of hints about what facilities for the elderly can do.
I thought that it would be very instructive to introduce Judson to Japanese people.

I write this book mainly by the extract of my notebook which I wrote during my stay at Judson in 1996 and 1997, by the centennial publication "Judson at University Circle 1906–2006, A Century of Excellence" and by material about CIP.

(4) ジュドソンの紹介をしたい

　2007年7月、ジュドソンでの研修のため私をアメリカへ招待してくれた団体、CIPUSA (Council of International Programs USA)の創立50周年を記念して、過去の各国からのCIP研修参加者の組織であるCIF(Council of International Fellowship)の世界会議がクリーブランドで開催され、私もお世話になった人々に会うためもあって参加した。

　その際ジュドソン・リタイアメント・コミュニティを再訪し、会長のシンシア・H・ダン女史に当時研修をとおして素晴らしい経験をさせていただいたことのお礼を述べた。

　ジュドソンについて日本に紹介したいとかねてから考えていたこともあり、そのことを述べたところ、会長から全面的協力の約束をもらうことができた。

　ジュドソンの考え方と活動・歴史を記した2006年出版の創立100周年記念誌にはジュドソンの歴史や活動が紹介され、ジュドソンの高いレベルのサービス活動を支えている信条・哲学ともいうべきものが明らかにされている。

　教えられることの多いすぐれた内容で、人が人生の後半を豊かに生きるための知恵と高齢者施設に何ができるかについての示唆が数多く含まれており、それを日本に紹介することは大きな意味があるのではないかと感じた。

　そのため主として私が1996、97年にジュドソンで経験し感じたことについての当時のノートからの抜き書きに、ジュドソン100年記念誌『ユニバーシティサークルにおけるジュドソン 1906－2006 卓越の一世紀』およびCIP関係資料によるCIPの紹介を交えて本書を書きたい。

(5) CIP (Council of International Programs)

In 1996 CIP invited me to the United States to study as an intern at Judson.
In 1956 Dr. Henry B. Ollendorff, a German lawyer organized CIP to invite foreign youth leaders and social workers for giving them the opportunity to study, work on the field and attend lectures to lift up the level of their professional skills and to extend cross-cultural exchange.

Since its foundation CIP has invited more than 10,000 participants from various countries to the USA. From Japan around 130 people have participated in this program since 1962.
Thanks to CIP, I had a very fruitful experience at Judson.

When I participated in the CIP program, the organization which invited me was called "Council of International Programs" (CIP).
But now it is known as and operating as "Council of International Programs USA" (CIPUSA).

(5) CIP（カウンシル・オブ・インターナショナル・プログラムズ）

　私がこの施設で学ぶことができたのは、CIPという団体がアメリカでの研修の機会を用意してくれたからであった。この団体はヒットラー時代初期のドイツで13か月獄に入れられた経験をした後、アメリカへ移住したドイツの法律家ヘンリー・B・オレンドルフ博士が、青少年育成や社会福祉等対人サービス従事者をアメリカに招き、実習トレーニング・講義等を通じて、対人サービス従事者の向上・異文化交流に寄与しようと1956年に創設した団体である。創立以来50年の間に世界147カ国から10,000人を超える人々をアメリカに招き研修と相互理解の場を提供してきている。日本からも1962年以来約130名が参加している。

　CIPのおかげでジュドソンでの実り多い経験をすることができた。

　私がCIP研修に参加したときには、私を招いてくれた団体はカウンシル・オブ・インターナショナル・プログラムズ(CIP)と呼ばれていた。しかし現在は、カウンシル・オブ・インターナショナル・プログラムズ USA (CIPUSA)と呼ばれ、その名で事業をすすめている。

Part One: What do we need to live our lives with satisfaction?

2. CIP chose Judson for me to study as an intern

(1) Participate in the CIP program

In 1996 I was an administrator of a facility of social welfare for the elderly as I wrote. I sent an application of the CIP program to the Japanese National Committee of the International Council on Social Welfare, which cooperated then with CIP to select and subsidize the participants in the CIP program.
CIPUSA is an organization as follows:
"CIPUSA is a non-profit international educational exchange program. It is committed to promoting international understanding through professional development and cross-cultural exchange. CIPUSA provides programs for individuals and groups in social services, non-profit, business and public organizations." (Home Page of CIPUSA, 15 May 2009)
According to the pamphlet then of the Japanese National Committee of the International Council on Social Welfare for application to the CIP program in 1996, the CIP programs are put into practice at more than 10 branches in the United States. The participants learn the social welfare services and so forth in the United States through lectures, discussions and trainings. At the same time this program promotes international understanding and cross-cultural exchange, contributing for world peace.
(The Japanese National Committee of the International Council on Social Welfare finished cooperation with the program. So the number of recent CIP participants from Japan is small now.)

2 CIPは私の研修先として
　ジュドソンを選んでくれた

(1) CIP 研修への参加

　1996年、前述したように当時高齢者福祉施設の管理者を務めていた私が参加したアメリカでのCIP国際研修に関しては、社団法人国際社会福祉協議会日本国委員会が日本からの参加者選考・助成を行っていた。
　CIPUSAは次のように紹介されている。
「CIPUSAは非営利の国際的教育交流プログラムである。職業的能力向上と異文化交流を通して国際理解の増進につとめている。CIPはソーシャルサービス・非営利・ビジネスや公的組織の個人・グループに対するプログラムを提供している」（CIPUSAのホームページ2009.5.15より）
　国際社会福祉協議会日本国委員会の海外派遣事業のパンフレット「社会福祉従事者のための国際研修プログラム（CIP）参加候補者募集要項（1996年派遣）」によると、このプログラムはアメリカ国内の10以上の支部で行われ、講義・討論・実習等によってアメリカの社会福祉サービス等の実態を知らせ、併せて海外諸国からの参加者との国際的文化交流・相互理解を推進し、ひいては世界平和を達成することを目的とするものとなっている。
（その後国際社会福祉協議会日本国委員会による助成と窓口の役割が終了したため、その後の日本からの参加者は少なくなっている）

　上記要項によると応募資格の主なものは、民間・行政各部門の社会福祉等の分野に従事する者で、専門的実践的にたずさわり、過去2年以上の勤務経験を有することと、専門分野において交流ができる英会話能力を有する者というものであった。
　私の属する法人の研修計画の一環として申し込んだ。

The pamphlet says that the application is open to those people as follows:
① Having been professionally and practically engaged in social welfare and so on in a private or administrative field for more than 2 years
② Having English speaking ability enough to communicate in the special field
I applied for it through the study plan of the organization in which I was working.

I was interviewed in English about my work and what I wanted to study in the United States at the Japanese National Committee of the International Council on Social Welfare.
Three, including me, were chosen as the participants among the applicants.
Thus I participated in the CIPUSA program.

(2) Departure

The plane arrived at Cleveland International Airport in Ohio via Detroit from Narita in November 1996.
The other two participants from Japan left Japan in August. But I left Japan in November because of the convenience of Judson.
At the Cleveland Airport some people of CIPUSA welcomed me.
From my arrival to Cleveland I was very busy for four months. I studied as an intern at Judson, attended the lectures and discussions at CIP, attended the lectures at Case Western Reserve University, attended the meetings with the other participants from various countries for cross-cultural exchange,

全国社会福祉協議会の建物内にある申し込み窓口の国際社会福祉協議会日本国委員会で、従事する仕事に関する質問やアメリカで何を学びたいか等について英語による面接があった。何倍かの申込者があったが、その年は3名が参加できることになり、私もその中に含まれていた。
　このようにして私はCIP研修に参加することになった。

(2) 出発

　1996年11月、飛行機は成田からアメリカのデトロイトを経由してオハイオ州クリーブランド国際空港に到着した。私以外の2名の日本からの参加者は8月に出発していたが、私の場合は受け入れ先の都合により11月末の到着となった。空港にはCIP関係者が出迎えてくれた。
　その後4カ月の間、盛りだくさんのプログラム参加で忙しく過ごすことになった。CIPの用意してくれた研修施設での実習のほか、CIPによる講義・討論・研究集会やケース・ウエスタンリザーブ大学での受講、各国からの参加者との異文化交流、参加者の宿泊している各ホストファミリーとの交流集会やマイノリティ問題に関する市民集会等々への参加があった。
　各国からの参加者は、CIPの講義やその他のいくつかのプログラ

Part One: What do we need to live our lives with satisfaction?

attended the meeting with host families of the participants, attended the civil meeting to debate minority issue and so forth.
The participants attended the CIP lectures and some other programs together. We participants studied as interns at different places which CIP had chosen according to the wishes of the respective participants.
My wish about my study as an intern was as follows:
① to study the management of facilities for the elderly
② to study the practical works there
③ to study the ways to raise subscriptions for social welfare
④ to study how to get better cooperation from volunteers

CIP chose Judson Retirement Community as the most suitable place for me to study.

CIP kindly endeavored to realize the wishes of the respective participants as much as possible.
According to my wish, I could attend the class of Prof. Binstock about "American Public Policy and Aging", and the seminar of Prof. D. Hammark about "American Social Policy since 1900", both once a week (2 hours) for 3 months at the post graduate course in Case Western Reserve University which was founded in 1826.
The participants stay at the host families' as home-stays. I stayed at 4 host families', one month each. Home stay is given a very important place in the CIP program to develop mutual understanding through the experiences of American civil life. It was really a wonderful experience for me.

I will write more about CIP in Part Three.

ムには共に出席するが、実習は個別にそれぞれの参加者の希望を聞いてCIPが選んでくれる。

　私の場合は、仕事との関係の深いテーマ、①高齢者施設の経営、②そこでの各職種の実務、③社会福祉事業に対する募金の方法、④ボランティア受け入れの方法、を学びたいと希望を提出しておいた。

　それにふさわしい研修の場としてCIPが用意してくれたのがクリーブランド市にある高齢者複合施設ジュドソン・リタイアメント・コミュニティであった。

　この研修ではCIPが参加者の希望をできる限り実現できるよう取りはからってくれ、私の場合は私の希望に従ってクリーブランドのケース・ウエスタンリザーブ大学（1826年創立の伝統ある大学である）での大学院のR.ビンストック教授の講義「アメリカの公共政策と高齢化」と同大学院のD.ハマック教授のゼミ「1900年以後のアメリカの社会政策」にそれぞれ週1回（2時間）、3か月間出席することができ、盛り沢山の研修となった。

　また、研修参加者はCIPの用意してくれるホームステイ先に宿泊することになっており、私の場合は約1か月毎に合計4軒のホームステイ先に宿泊した。ホームステイはアメリカの市民生活の体験を通して相互理解を深めるものとして、CIP研修において特に重要な位置づけを与えられている。私にとってホームステイはすばらしい経験であった。

　CIPについては第3部で詳しく述べる。

(3) Judson is in Cleveland

Judson is situated in Cleveland on the south coast of Lake Erie in Northern Ohio, Middle West part of the United States.
The population of Cleveland is about half a million and that of Greater Cleveland (including the surrounding area) is about 2 million.
Cleveland developed as a city of steel and machinery. Now it is famous for Cleveland Indians of the Major League of baseball, the Cleveland Orchestra and so on.

Judson has two big facilities for the elderly now. The one is Judson Park with the corporate head office at University Circle near Case Western Reserve University. And the other is 10 storied Judson Manor, the former gorgeous hotel about one kilometer from Judson Park. And the corporation is now building the third facility campus, South Franklin Circle in the suburbs of Cleveland.

At Judson Park, there is a 6 storied building and a 10 storied building.
In the 6 storied building, there is the corporate head office, rooms for Alzheimer residents on the second floor, a general nursing home on the 4th floor, Bruening Health Center for both moderate and advanced dementia on the 5th floor and a skilled nursing home on the 6th floor. There is also a rehabilitation room, medical offices and so on.

There is a big pool both for the residents of Judson and for the people in the neighborhood. It is used for rehabilitation, health support programs and so forth.

(3) ジュドソンはクリーブランドにある

　ジュドソン・リタイアメント・コミュニティは、アメリカ中西部オハイオ州の北部にあり、エリー湖の南岸に面したクリーブランド市にある。クリーブランド市は人口約50万だが、近郊を含めた広域クリーブランド（グレイタークリーブランド）は約200万人が住む地域である。かつては鉄鋼・機械等重工業が盛んであったが、今ではアメリカ大リーグのクリーブランドインディアンスやクリーブランドオーケストラ等で有名である。

　ジュドソンは2つの大きな高齢者施設を持っている。ケース・ウエスタンリザーブ大学の近く、ユニバーシティサークルと呼ばれる地域に、法人本部のある「ジュドソンパーク」と呼ばれる高齢者複合施設がある。そこから1キロメートルほど離れた所に元豪華ホテルであった10階建てのもう1つの施設「ジュドソンメナー」がある。さらに現在は2009年開設を目指してクリーブランド近郊に第3の施設「サウスフランクリンサークル」を建設中である。

　ジュドソンパークには、広い敷地に主な建物として、6階建ての棟とそれに接続した10階建ての棟がある。6階建ての本部のある建物には、2階に軽いアルツハイマー病のレジデントのための居室があり、4階はジェネラルナーシングホームと呼ばれ、ケアを要するレジデントのための居室がある。5階はブリューニングヘルスセンターと呼ばれる軽度及び重度の認知症レジデントの居室、6階はスキルドナーシング（医療的な処置の必要なレジデントのための）居室となっている。その他リハビリ室・医務室等がある。
　また大きなプールもあり、施設のレジデント以外にも、近隣からのリハビリのための利用者や健康プログラム参加者の受け入れ等に使われている。
　その建物に接続して、インデペンデントリビングといわれる自立レジデントの居室と、アシステッドリビングといわれる要支援レジデントの居室がある10階建ての建物がある。

Near this building, there is a 10 storied building of apartments both for independent living and assisted living.

There is a big mansion named Bicknell Mansion which was used for day enrichment service when I studied in 1996 and 1997.

Later the day enrichment center was moved to Judson Manor.

When I visited Judson again in 2007, the mansion was used for gorgeous rooms of independent living.

(4) Judson Manor

Judson Manor was a 10 storied gorgeous hotel with a penthouse on the top. The carpet on its corridor is the same one used when the Manor was a hotel. It still keeps fresh color. The Manor creates a splendid atmosphere.

The rooms are used both for independent living and independent living with assistance.

When they want to use plural rooms personally, Judson prepares the rooms as they want. The residents take a meal at the restaurant in an atmosphere like a hotel.

They can cook by themselves at Judson Park and Judson Manor when they want to.

第1部 人生を豊かに生きるために必要なものは何か

　本部の建物から少し離れて古いマンション（大邸宅の建物）があり、私が1996、97年に研修した時にはデイエンリッチメント（デイサービス）に使われていたが、その後デイエンリッチメントはジュドソンメナーに移り、2007年に再訪した時にはマンションは改修されて、インデペンデントリビングの豪華な居室に変わっていた。

(4) ジュドソンメナー

　ジュドソンメナーは10階建てで、屋上にペントハウスが付いており、もと豪華なホテルだったところである。じゅうたんも元のホテル時代のものが使われているということだが、色も鮮やかなままであった。

　豪華ホテルの雰囲気そのままである。部屋は自立者のためのインデペンデントリビングと（軽度の）支援を要する自立者用に使われており、希望に応じて複数室をまとめて1人のための居室用に改修してもらえる。食事はホテルのような雰囲気のレストランで食べる。パーク、メナーとも希望により自炊もできる。

ジュドソンメナーのレストラン
Restaurant of Judson Manor.

Part One: What do we need to live our lives with satisfaction?

3. Working together

(1) To study many fields of works

Judson accepted my wish to study as many fields of works at Judson as possible. I could study and work at many areas in it.

When I finished my stay for 4 months at Judson, Ms. Cynthia Dunn, President & CEO of Judson, handed over to me the paper of conclusion of my training. The paper said as follows:

The following list specially identified the areas he covered.
Volunteer Services, Day Enrichment, Recreational Therapy, Aquatic Therapy, Dining Services, Security and Transportation, Judson Manor Assisted Living, Plant Management, Maintenance, Finance, Social Services, Human Resources, Development, Occupational Therapy, Marketing and Sales, Admissions, Home Health Care, Health Maintenance, Nursing, Judson Park Assisted Living, Judson Manor Administration, Alzheimer Unit, Judson Park Administration, Medical Office.

I got familiar not only with the management and the staff but also with some of the residents. Some residents invited me to their rooms, telling about their daily lives at Judson and teaching me what I should pay attention to in American life.
I travelled for one week to the East Coast of the United States. When I started, some residents advised me to be careful not to have money or bags stolen.
As I wrote, a resident showed me the files of the autobiographies of some tens of the residents. She asked me how to

第1部 人生を豊かに生きるために必要なものは何か

3 共に働く

(1) 多くの部署の働きを学ぶ

　ジュドソンでは、出来るだけ多くの職場の部署での仕事を体験したいという私の希望を受け入れてくれ、多くの部署で職員とともに働き、仕事の実際を体験することができた。4か月の研修終了にあたり、ジュドソンのシンシア・ダン会長から手渡された研修終了証には、私が研修体験した部署は次の通りであると書かれていた。

　ボランティアサービス、デイエンリッチメント（デイサービス）、リクリエーションセラピー、アクアティックセラピー（水中療法）、食事サービス、セキュリティと送迎、ジュドソンメナーのアシステッドリビング（要支援棟）、施設維持管理、財務、ソーシャルサービス（相談業務）、人事、施設開発、作業療法、マーケティングとセールス、入所担当、在宅ヘルスケア、健康管理、看護、ジュドソンパークのアシステッドリビング、ジュドソンメナーの運営管理、アルツハイマー棟、ジュドソンパークの運営管理、医務

　その間、管理職やスタッフだけでなく、レジデントの何人かとも親しくなれた。レジデントの中には個室に招いてくれたり、ジュドソンでの生活について話してくれたり、アメリカ生活について注意すべきことを教えてくれた人もあった。
　途中でニューヨーク等東海岸の大都会に1週間旅行したが、大都会には危険が多いので財布等貴重品は肌身離さず持ち、荷物は手から離さないようになどの忠告をしてくれた。
　先にも書いたが、あるレジデントは、自分がまとめている何十人かのレジデントの自分史のファイルを見せてくれ、これをどのよう

make good use of them.

She was near 90 years old. She was leading a very active life at Judson, practicing to learn how to handle a personal computer, and serving as a conductor of the hand bell club of Judson.

Another resident was guiding visitors joyfully with a name card as a volunteer.

I was deeply impressed by the active work of the staff and the lively living of the residents with satisfaction and in their own character.

(2) Difference between the two countries

I touch on a difference of the position of facilities for the elderly in local communities in the United States and Japan.

In Japan local governments such as cities, towns or villages are sometimes reluctant to have more facilities for the elderly. I didn't hear such a case in the United States.

In Japan local governments have to take on more financial burden on social insurance both of public long-term care insurance for people from 40 years old and of health insurance for the elderly from 75 years old as a general rule when the number of the elderly increases. Local governments have to shoulder a part of the cost of social insurance both of public long-term care insurance and of health insurance for the elderly.

In the United States they have medicare for the elderly from 65years old and for people with disabilities, and medicaid for

に生かせばよいか等の意見を求められた。このレジデントは90近い歳だったが、パソコンを習い、レジデントのハンドベルクラブの指揮者を務めたりで、大変積極的な生活を送っている人だった。

また、あるレジデントは胸にボランティアという名札を付け、嬉々として来客への応対をしていた。

ジュドソンでは、職員の熱意ある働きと、レジデントの満足げなのびのびした生活ぶりに感銘を受けた。

(2) 日本とのちがい

地域社会との関係で、高齢者施設のおかれた立場がアメリカと日本でどのように違うかについて一点触れておきたい。

日本では市町村のような地方自治体が高齢者施設の増加に反対することがある。アメリカではこの種の話は全く聞かなかった。

日本では地方自治体で高齢者の数が増えると、社会保険である40歳以上の国民を対象とする介護保険及び原則として75歳以上の国民を対象とする老人保健に関し、市町村の財政上の負担が増える。市町村は介護保険及び老人保健の費用の一部を負担することになっているからである。

これに対し、アメリカでは連邦政府と被保険者が費用を負担する65歳以上の高齢者と障害者に対する高齢者医療保険制度メディケア、連邦政府と州政府が折半で費用を負担する低所得者医療扶助制度メディケイドがある。しかしカウンティ（日本の県にあたる）や市町村のような地方自治体はメディケア及びメディケイドに対し財政上の負担はしない。

people who need public aids because of low income and for people with disabilities. In case of medicare the Federal Government and the insured bear the expences. In case of medicaid the Federal Government and each state bear the expences. Local governments such as counties, cities, towns or villages are not responsible financially for medicare and medicaid.

In Japan in ordinary case, for local governments to have more facilities for the elderly means to take on more financial burden of public long-term care insurance and health insurance for the elderly. That's why local governments in Japan are sometimes reluctant to have more facilities for the elderly.

第1部 人生を豊かに生きるために必要なものは何か

　日本では通常の場合、高齢者施設が増えることは介護保険・老人保健に関し市町村の財政的負担が増加することを意味する。そのため市町村のような地方自治体がときとして高齢者施設が増えることに反対することが起こるのである。

Part One: What do we need to live our lives with satisfaction?

4. Task of Social Work Department

(1) About the fee

On the desk of the Director of Social Work there are the photos of her children and husband in a small frame. On the wall behind her, the official license of social worker is hung.
She taught me the task of social work department.

When someone wants to be a resident of independent living or assisted living of Judson, it must be confirmed that he or she can afford the fee through life.
If he or she cannot pay the fee later for some reasons, Judson will pay. He or she can have spending money even in such case. They have this system, so residents need not leave Judson halfway.
Residents get medical care by private health insurance or medicare from 65 years old. Medicaid for low income groups can be utilized if there is a condition of it.

Residents want to live in the independent living as long as possible.
The reason is:
1. the wish of the residents
2. Judson's philosophy that it wants the residents live independently as long as possible
3. the wish of the families of the residents

The wish of the families is as follows:
1. They wish the residents to live in their own character independently and with dignity

40

第1部 人生を豊かに生きるために必要なものは何か

4 ソーシャルワークの課題

(1) 費用負担について

　ソーシャルワーク室の部長のデスクの上には、お子さんと夫君の写真が小さな額に入れて飾られており、壁にはソーシャルワーカーの資格を証明する免許状が飾られている。部長に仕事について聞いた。

　自立棟（インデペンデントリビング）、要支援棟（アシステッドリビング）の利用については、一生継続して施設利用ができる費用を賄えるかを確認して入居してもらうことになるが、万一何らかの事情で後にそれがかなわなくなった場合でも、法人で補助する制度があるので、途中で退去することは必要ではない。自分のおこずかいを残して、足らない分は当法人で負担することになる。
　医療については、私的医療保険のほかに、65歳になれば高齢者医療保険制度のメディケアを利用できる。その他場合によっては低所得者のための医療扶助制度のメディケイドを利用するケースもある。

　レジデントは、できる限り長く自立棟で生活したいという希望を持つ。
　主な理由は3つあると考えられる。①本人の希望、②レジデントにできるだけ長く自立生活を続けてほしいという当法人のフィロソフィー、③家族の希望。

　家族の希望には主に、①できる限り長く自分らしく自立し尊厳をもって生きてほしい、②自分のことができないと本人にとっても子供たち家族にとっても敗北感につながりやすいので、できる限り自立した生活を続けてもらいたい　という2つの理由が考えられる。

　このような中で、ジュドソンのレジデントは、引退後もアクティ

41

Part One: What do we need to live our lives with satisfaction?

2. They don't want the residents and the families themselves to have the feeling of failure.

Many residents want to continue their active lives after retirement. A lot of residents act outside Judson. Some study at university auditing classes, some work as part-time workers, some work as volunteers for social service activities and so forth.

ブに生きたいという希望を強く持っている人が多い。大学の聴講生として勉強したり、パートタイムで働いたり、ボランティアとして社会奉仕活動などをしたりして外部での活動を積極的に行う人も多い。

ジュドソンメナーの屋上から
From the rooftop of Judson Manor.

(2) When they get weaker

One of the important principles of Judson is as follows:
They have to have careful consideration that the residents can move to the facility of the weaker level without the feeling of failure when they get weaker.
When residents have to change from independent living to assisted living, social workers, nurses and some other staff have a discussion and listen to the wishes of the residents to decide whether the change is necessary.
They decide the change by consultation with the staff present. They have the meeting for the consultation once every two months.
When they can't wait for the next meeting, they decide the change before they have the next meeting.
In the case of Alzheimer or dementia, the families are often unable to accept the situation. In such case they talk with the families until they get understanding. The cooperation of social workers and nurses is very important.

As to the service of the day enrichment center, formerly they only accepted those who paid the fee by themselves. But now they accept many people who get public aid for the service to contribute to the local community.
They get services by the so called Passport Program, without any personal charge. If they have to pay personally for some reasons, Judson pays for them.

(2) 体力が弱ってきたとき

　ジュドソンの方針中の重要なものの一つに、体力が衰えてきたときにレジデントが敗北感を持たずに次のレベルに移っていけるように配慮しつとめることがある。自立棟から要支援棟へレベルを替える場合には、ソーシャルワーカー、看護師のほかケアワーカー等他職種も加わってレジデントの希望を聞き、出席職員の合議でレベル変更が必要かを決定する。2か月に1回の会なのでどうしてもそれまで待てない場合には、会議を開く前に替ってもらうこともある。
　アルツハイマーや認知症のケースは家族にとって受け入れることが困難な場合が多いので、家族に来てもらってよく話し合う。その場合、ソーシャルワーカーと看護師の協力が特に重要である。

　デイエンリッチメント（デイサービス）利用者については、当初は費用負担ができる人を対象にしていたが、今は地域社会への貢献を重視し、州から県（カウンティ）に委託されている公的扶助による利用者を多く受け入れている。その人たちは公費による負担で本人負担なしのいわゆるパスポート（利用券）でサービス利用をしているが、万一その他に費用がかかる場合には当法人が負担している。

Part One: What do we need to live our lives with satisfaction?

5. Reminiscence Hour

(1) Reminiscence as psychotherapy

Aunt Ann is a retired social worker of Judson. She was serving as a volunteer of "reminiscence hour" to the residents at Judson.
"The reminiscence hour" was held on the 5th floor of Judson Park where Bruening Health Center was.
The residents in mild and moderate condition attended there.

Reminiscence therapy is the psychotherapy for the elderly originated by psychiatrist R.N. Butler.
It assists and sustains the elderly by helping them recollect their past lives, search for and confirm the meaning of their lives.
It aims to help the elderly cope with their inner problems by themselves. It is one of the most widespread psychotherapies that remove the oppressed feeling by helping them take their lives affirmatively and hold their self-respect. (*)

The way of reminiscence hour by Aunt Ann was not exactly the same of that of Butler. She placed current topics one after another and brought out interest and energy from the elderly.

One day, eight residents were present. Aunt Ann spoke loudly to be heard by the elderly.

The topics she placed were as follows:

5 回想法の時間

(1) 心理療法としての回想法

　アンおばさんはジュドソンの退職したソーシャルワーカーである。ボランティアとして回想法の時間にジュドソンのレジデントに奉仕している。回想法の時間は、ブリューニングヘルスセンターのある5階で開かれ、軽度から重度手前の高齢者が参加していた。

　回想法は、精神科医のバトラーによって始められた主に高齢者を対象とする心理療法である。高齢者が自らの人生を振り返り、人生の意味や価値を模索し、問い直すことによって、高齢者自身が心の問題に取り組んでいくことを支援していくものである。人生を肯定的にとらえ、自尊心を高めることにより高齢者の抑うつ気分を緩和する心理療法として最も広く普及しているものの一つである。※

　アンおばさんの回想法の方法は、必ずしもバトラーの心理療法に正確に従ったものではないが、次々と最近の話題を提供し、出席者の興味と元気を引き出していた。

　その日は8人が参加していた。アンおばさんは皆によく聴こえるような大きな声で話した。

　70年代に宇宙へ人類が初めて行った話。
　ニューヨークの犯罪件数が減りました。アトランタより犯罪比率

Part One: What do we need to live our lives with satisfaction?

The story that human-being went first to the outer space.

The number of crimes in New York has diminished. The percentage of crime in New York is less than that of Atlanta. It is the result of the effort of New York that it trained policemen and investigated what kinds of crimes were increasing.

The hostages in the Japanese Embassy in Peru decreased to 83. (Then it was the time of the hostage incident in Peru.)

It snowed a lot and stormed in Seattle.

The hot controversy is going on in California about teaching Black English in public schools. Black English is called Ebonics.

Suddenly Aunt Ann asked me whether such controversy was in Japan. I replied that there were dialects in Japan, but was no controversy about teaching dialects in schools.

We celebrated the two hundred year anniversary of Cleveland.

In 1999 we will have a new football team.

In 1996 there was the election of US president.

Four top men and women of the year were named "Person of the Year" by Time Magazine. One is an Asian American who invented the medicine to treat HIV.

The serious problem now in America is that of drug and

第1部 人生を豊かに生きるために必要なものは何か

が下になりました。警官を訓練し、どういう犯罪が増えているかの調査を行うなど努力した結果です。

ペルーの日本大使館の人質が83人に減りました（当時はペルー人質事件のあった時期である）。

シアトルに大雪が降り、雪あらしになりました。

カリフォルニア州で黒人独特の英語（当時「イボニックス」と呼ばれるようになっていた）を公立学校で教えるべきか、今熱い議論が続いています。

そばで聞いていた私に突然アンおばさんは「日本でもこういう議論がありますか？」と聞いてきた。「日本にも方言がありますが、学校で方言を教えるべきという議論はありません」と答えた。

クリーブランドは200年祭を祝いました。
1999年に新しいフットボールチームができます。
1996年に大統領選挙がありました。
今年の話題の男女4人がタイムマガジンで発表されました。男女のうち1人はエイズの薬を発明したアジア系アメリカ人です。
今社会で深刻な問題は麻薬（ドラッグ）とアルコールです。日本でも同様の問題がありますかと私にたずねた。「日本でも麻薬とアルコールは深刻な問題になっています」と答えた。
今年亡くなった有名人は誰でしょう。

アンおばさんはこのように矢継ぎ早に話しかけていた。参加者はそのとおりと言ったり、驚きの声を上げたりで、感情の交流と高揚感が感じられた。参加者が関心を共有できる話題を提供し、連帯感を持てるような配慮がなされていた。

※黒川由紀子『回想法―高齢者の心理療法』［誠信書房、2005年］20～23頁

alcohol.
She asked me whether the same kind of problem was there in Japan.
I replied that the problem of drug and alcohol was serious in Japan, too.

Who are the famous persons that died this year?

Aunt Ann spoke speedily. The participants replied "Yes" or reacted in an astonishing voice. There were exchange of feeling and uplift of sentiment. She offered topics which the participants could hold in common and have a sense of solidarity in.

(*) Kurokawa Yukiko, "Reminiscence—Psychological Therapy for the Elderly" (in Japanese) (Seishin Shobo, 2005), pp. 20-23

(2)Reminiscence hour on another day

Ten residents were present.

Who was appointed the Secretary of State?

Do you know about the blizzard in New England?

FBI decided to offer a reward for the information on the offender who threw a bomb at the Atlanta Olympic Games.

Influenza is epidemic this year. Many people have received flu shot.

(2) 別の日の回想法の時間

　10人のレジデントが出席していた。

　誰が国務長官に指名されましたか？
　ニューイングランド州の大吹雪を知っていますか？
　アトランタオリンピックで爆弾を投げた犯人についての情報提供者にFBIが懸賞金を出すことを決めました。
　今年はインフルエンザが流行っています。予防接種を受けた人も多いですね。
　昔のバンドのベニーグッドマンやルイアームストロングを知っていますか？　有名なバンドの前で踊ったことがありますか？（4～5人が手を挙げた）

Part One: What do we need to live our lives with satisfaction?

Do you know the bands like Benny Goodman or Louis Armstrong?
Did you dance in front of famous bands?
Four or five residents raised hands.

People danced to a boogie-woogie and so on, didn't they?

Who has lived in Cleveland long?
Three or four residents raised hands.

Do you know the songs of Pattie Page? Do you know the song of "Tennesee Waltz"? Do you know Rosemary Clooney?
Do you know the song of "Come onna my house"? This is the photo of her in young days. She had many children.

Kate Smith sang the American classic, "God bless America".

Do you know Dinah Shore? She sang "Moon River".

Do you know the signature song of Frank Sinatra? It is "My way", isn't it?

Later, Aunt Ann told me that she chose topics from magazines and so forth.

第1部 人生を豊かに生きるために必要なものは何か

　ブギウギなどで踊りましたね。
　昔からクリーブランドに住んでいた人は？（3〜4人が手を挙げた）
　パティーページの歌を知っていますか？　テネシーワルツを知っていますか？　ローズマリークルーニーを知っていますか？　カモンナマイハウスという歌を知っていますか？　ここに若い時の写真があります。彼女にはたくさんの子供がいます。
　ケイトスミスはアメリカクラシック曲の「ゴッドブレスアメリカ」を歌いました。
　ダイナショアを知っていますか？　ムーンリバーを歌っています。
　フランクシナトラのシグネチュアソングを知っていますか？　マイウエイですね。

　アンおばさんは、話題は雑誌などから探していると、後で食事のときに話してくれた。

Part One: What do we need to live our lives with satisfaction?

6. At Day Enrichment Center

(1) The activity

During my stay at Judson as an intern the Day Enrichment service was offered at Bicknell Mansion. Afterwards it was moved to Judson Manor.

Activity
The center is open from 8:30 a.m. to 5:00 p.m.
Transportation is entrusted to a private company.

The chief of the center works from 9:00 a.m. to 5:00 p.m.
Three staff work from 8:30 a.m. to 4:30 p.m.
The full quota of the participants per a day is 24.
One day the number of participants was 18.

A part of participants pay the fee by themselves. Participants of low income groups get the service for nothing, by the so called Passport Program offered by the State.
The majority of the participants are using the Passport Program.
The number of the registered participants is 37. Normally, from 18 to 20 participants come in a day.

(2) The program

One day the program is as follows:
1. breakfast from 9:00 to 11:00 a.m., bread baked with butter and coffee
2. playing a quiz game

6 デイサービスセンターにて

(1) 活動

　私の研修時には、パークの本部ビルの近くにあるビックネルマンションでデイサービスが行われていたが、その後メナーへ場所替えとなったことはすでに述べた。

活動
　朝8時30分から午後5時まで開く。送迎は外部の会社が請け負っている。

　　朝9時〜午後5時　主任の勤務時間
　　8時30分〜4時30分　スタッフ3名の勤務時間
　　1日の定員　24人
　　この日は18人の参加

　一部の人は自費参加だが、低所得者の場合は州政府の負担で通称パスポートと呼ばれる無料券でサービスを受ける。パスポート利用者が多数である。
　全体の登録者数は37人だが、通常1日18〜20人が参加する。

(2) ある日のプログラム

　ある日のプログラムはつぎのとおりである。
　9時〜11時　朝食（パンのバター焼きとコーヒー）
　その後　クイズ遊び
　職員による新聞の読み聞かせ

3. reading aloud newspapers by the staff

On a certain day I was deeply impressed by a talk of a staff at this hour.

The staff was an African American.
Her talk was as follows:
There still remains slavery in North Africa, Sudan and the Gulf countries. A newspaper reports that slaves of the area wish for help from the United States. In America, there was also slavery until president Abraham Lincoln abolished it in the middle of 19th century.
America is a young country, but we enjoy the high level of life and freedom here. I have visited Europe. But I prefer America.

My comment:
Ohio is famous for its "Underground Railway".
In the days of slavery, many slaves tried to flee to Canada where they could get freedom. Many of them fled to Canada through Ohio. A lot of volunteers in Ohio helped slaves flee to Canada in secret. It was called "Underground Railway".

Other talks from topics of newspaper.
A newspaper reports about the plan to build a garbage dump for New York in Ohio.
We don't like such a plan, do you?

Other topic:
There rises an uproar when it snows in southern states. They don't take measures to get rid of snow there.

第1部 人生を豊かに生きるために必要なものは何か

　ある日、私は職員の話に強い印象を受けた。その職員はアフリカ系アメリカ人であった。

《職員の話》
　北アフリカやスーダンまた湾岸諸国では今も奴隷制が残っていて、それらの人々からアメリカに助けを求めてきているという新聞記事がある。
　アメリカでも19世紀半ばにエブラハムリンカーン大統領が廃止するまで奴隷制度があった。アメリカは若い国だが、生活水準も高く自由もある。私はヨーロッパに行ったことがあるが、私はアメリカが好きです。

《私のコメント》
　オハイオ州はいわゆる「地下鉄道」で有名である。アメリカに奴隷制度があった時代に多くの奴隷が自由を得られるカナダへ逃れようと試みた。その多くがオハイオ経由で逃亡した。オハイオには多くのボランティアにより彼らをひそかにカナダまで送り届ける運動があった。これを「アンダーグラウンドレイルウエイ（地下鉄道）」と呼んだ。

別の記事について
　ニューヨークのごみ処理場をここオハイオ州に作る案が新聞に出ている。皆さんも嫌でしょう？

他の記事
　南部の州では雪が少しでも降ると大騒ぎになる。雪対策が立てられていないから。

　単に大きな声で新聞記事の内容を紹介するだけでなく、職員の受け取り方、考えも紹介していたことが新鮮に感じられた。

Part One: What do we need to live our lives with satisfaction?

I felt very fresh because the staff read aloud topics from newspapers and at the same time told their own opinion about them.

11:30 a.m.
physical exercise with music

At noon
lunch at the restaurant of Judson Park
gorgeous and voluminous lunch

In the afternoon
watching a movie

On other day
A staff was talking about jokes.
What day is the strong day in a week?
The answer is Saturday and Sunday.
The reason is:
Other days are weekdays (weak days).

I had strong impression by the active reaction of the participants.

第1部 人生を豊かに生きるために必要なものは何か

ジュドソンパークの玄関
Entrance of Judson Park.

11時30分
（別の部屋で）テープの音楽に合わせて体操。

12時
　パークの食堂で昼食　豪華なごちそうだ。私など食べられないほどのボリューム。

　午後は映画観賞

別の日のこと
　職員がレジデントにジョークについて話していた。
　What day is the strong day in a week?　(週のどの日が強い日ですか？)
　答えは土曜と日曜。他の日はウイークデイ（弱い日）だから、というようなジョーク。利用者の活発な反応が印象的だった。

Part One: What do we need to live our lives with satisfaction?

7. From the Chief Financial Officer

The Chief Financial Officer (CFO) is a certified public accountant (CPA) and worked at a hospital and in an auditing corporation. He was invited to Judson as its CFO.

He told me the issues they were facing.

The Judson Services, Inc. carries on the enterprise independently, getting no aid from any other organization.
The corporation is a not-for-profit organization, receiving official preferential treatment of taxation.
On the other hand, special considerations on the enterprise are required.

When the residents start to live at Judson, it must be confirmed that they can afford their fees at Judson through their lives. If residents need lawyers for management of their own property, Judson introduces lawyers to them.

We are anxious that we will face serious situation of acquisitions and mergers as medical corporations are now facing.
There were many medical organizations in Cleveland before. Now there are only a few because of acquisitions and mergers by profit medical corporations.
Because of the development of Managed Care Organizations, medical corporations are now forced to grow bigger to survive.
We are afraid that this trend is coming to us.

7 最高財務責任者に聞く

　ジュドソンの最高財務責任者（Chief Financial Officer）は公認会計士の資格を持ち、病院や監査法人で仕事をしていたが、招かれてジュドソンの最高財務責任者に就任した。彼は直面している課題について話してくれた。

　法人は、他のどの組織からの援助も受けることなく、自主独立経営を行っている。法人は、非営利組織なので税制上の優遇措置を受けている。その代り事業上特別の考慮を要求される面もある。
　入居に際し、レジデントが一生の費用を賄えるかを確認する。利用者本人の資産管理のために、必要である場合には弁護士に依頼する斡旋なども行っている。

　我々の業界は、医療分野で進んでいる合併・買収（M＆A）などの動きが、高齢者施設の業界にも及んでくるのではないかという深刻な問題に直面している。
　クリーブランドには多くの医療機関があったが、営利法人の医療機関に合併・買収されるなどして、今では少数の病院に集約されてしまった。
　マネジドケア組織MCO（Managed Care Organization）※の進展により、医療機関が生き残るためには大型化する以外に方法はない。この動きが我々の業界にも及んでくる恐れがある。

　買収等の危険にさらされるのを避けるため、クリーブランド地域の高齢者施設業界の協議会を作って対応について研究を進めている。
（現在ジュドソンはサウスフランクリンサークルという新しい施設を建設中で、自主独立の健全経営を続けている）

　※MCOは、アメリカで発達した民間の管理医療制度による組織。

Part One: What do we need to live our lives with satisfaction?

We founded the council of the corporations of retirement facilities for the elderly in Cleveland to study how to cope with this situation.
(Judson is now building a new campus, South Franklin Circle and keeping the independent management.)

第1部 人生を豊かに生きるために必要なものは何か

民間の医療保険会社との契約により被保険者である患者が医療を受けることができる医療機関が指定されるものが典型である。

ジュドソンメナーの玄関
Entrance of Judson Manor.

Part One: What do we need to live our lives with satisfaction?

8. Subject of Management

The Vice President of Judson Park talked me about the current subject of management.

There are many providers in the health care business. The competition is hard among providers. Mergers are going on in this field, too.

It is not unusual that care workers resign as is prevalent in this country.
We are endeavoring to keep needed workers.
People must be motivated to carry out a high level of work. So, the management has to endeavor to have the staff and workers feel recognized and duly treated.
The management staff often meet to discuss issues in groups from eight to ten members.
I don't meet the managers so often as before. I show them my general expectation and let them carry out their works on their own for responsibility and flexibility.
The managers have to be motivated before the staff get motivated.
We can't wait long to evaluate their works. I consider that time management is very important.

Facilities for the elderly are, in ordinary cases, smaller in scale and the activity there is less speedy compared with hospitals. But both in facilities for the elderly and in hospitals many specialized professionals cooperate and work together in an integrated system.

8 経営管理上の考慮

経営管理上の関心事についてジュドソンパーク担当副会長に聞いた。

ヘルスケア業界の事業者は多く、競争は激しい。この業界でも合併が進行している。

ケアワーカーに中途退職者がかなり出るが、この地方では普通のことなので、職員確保に努めている。

職員に質の高い仕事をしてもらうには、モチベーションを持てるようにすることが大切だ。そのためには職員が職場で認められ、正当に処遇されていると感じるよう経営側が努めなければならない。

マネジメントのスタッフについては、8～10人ぐらいのグループで仕事上の問題を考えてもらっている。私としては、以前のようにはマネジャーたちと頻繁に会うことはせず、一般的な期待を示し、各々の責任でフレクシブルに対応するよう任せている。マネジャーにはスタッフに先んじてモチベーションを高めてもらわなければならない。仕事に対する評価はあまり待ってはおれず、また時間のマネジメントを重視している。

高齢者施設は、病院と比べて通常規模が大きくなく、また仕事のペースがゆったりしているところが一般的な違いといえると思うが、いろんな専門職種が統合されたシステムの下で協力して働く点では同じである。

最近はマネジドケアの会社等を通して、新しい入居希望者が紹介

Part One: What do we need to live our lives with satisfaction?

Recently clients have been often introduced to us by a managed care agency. Residents sometimes have high level of requirements such as more rooms, gorgeous furniture and so forth. They wish for placement of social workers, doctors of geriatrics, fulfillment of activity programs and comfortable living environment like hotels.

The main concern of those who want to be residents of Judson is as follows:
They come to Judson while they are healthy, and they get the broad continuum of services of assistance and care when they need them.

We are facing business competition, so we plan to have intermediate office in the suburban area to offer home care services to the people there. (Now it is realized.)

(We can get more information about Judson Retirement Community in the following home page.
http://www.judsonretirement.org/)

されてくることも多い。より多くの部屋や、豪華な家具の希望のようなハイレベルの要求もときどきある。

ソーシャルワーカーや老年医学の専門医の配置、アクティビティプログラムの充実のほか、ホテルのような快適な環境が求められているといえる。

ここに入居したい人たちの最大の関心事は、元気な間に入居して、体が弱ってきても継続してそれぞれの時期に必要となる支援やケアを受けられるサービスの連続性にある。

同業者との競争があるので、近郊に中継基地としてのオフィスを作り、そこの住民にホームケアサービスの提供をしたい（それは現在実現されている）。

（ジュドソン・リタイアメント・コミュニティの詳しい情報はホームページで得ることができる。http://www.judsonretirement.org/）

温水プールにて
At the warm water pool.

第 2 部

ユニバーシティサークルにおけるジュドソン
1906―2006
卓越の一世紀

Part Two

Judson
at University Circle
1906–2006
A Century of Excellence

Part Two: Judson at University Circle 1906–2006 A Century of Excellence

Table of Contents

1. Preface 72
2. Introduction 76
3. It was Cleveland's Gilded Age... 78
4. Community Partner and Resource 92
5. The Heart and Soul 100
6. Leading with Compassion and Vision 116
7. Creating a Legacy 122
8. Building on Success 124
9. Epilogue 128

Written by Wendy A. Hoke
Edited by Robert M. Lucarelli

第2部 ユニバーシティサークルにおけるジュドソン 1906—2006 卓越の一世紀

第 2 部 目次

1 はしがき ……………………………………………………… 73
2 前置き ………………………………………………………… 77
3 それはクリーブランドの金色に輝く時代 …………………… 79
4 コミュニティパートナーと地域の資源としてのジュドソン… 93
5 心と魂 ………………………………………………………… 101
6 共感とビジョンをもって先頭に立つ ………………………… 117
7 次代に残すべきもの …………………………………………… 123
8 建設計画の成功の上に ………………………………………… 125
9 エピローグ …………………………………………………… 129

ウエンディ・A・ホーク著
ロバート・M・ルカレリ編

Part Two: Judson at University Circle 1906–2006 A Century of Excellence

1. Preface

Celebrating this milestone anniversary gave me pause to remember how for the last 35 years my life has been interwoven with Judson. The weaving began when my mother was a resident at the Manor and Park for 16 years. After her death, I stayed in touch with other residents as a volunteer shopper and visitor. Four years ago our wonderful memories and reality about our future helped my husband and me decide it was time to call Judson Park home.

It did not take long to adapt to the Judson lifestyle. We were, and continue to be, impressed by the effort made by so many to ensure our comfort and well-being. We feel it when President and CEO, Cynthia Dunn, takes time to stop and chat about how our life is going or when one of many helpful staff members untangles a frustrating problem.

At last I have time to delve into long-neglected interests and have a new perspective while taking my walks in the neighborhood. Before our move, walking was primarily for exercise, something squeezed in between other chores. Now those walks not only help me negotiate the bumps life puts in my path, but also provide time to pause and enjoy a view, make friends with a shaggy dog, listen to the birds or be touched by a breeze. What a luxury to have time to appreciate the beauty waiting to be noticed.

Sitting near one of the ancient trees in the garden, I find myself comparing it to our 100-year-old community. Just as

第2部 ユニバーシティサークルにおけるジュドソン 1906—2006 卓越の一世紀

1 はしがき

　この里程標となる100年祭を祝うにあたって、過去35年間、私の人生がジュドソンと深い関わりを持ってきたことを思い返しています。
　ジュドソンとの関わりは、私の母がジュドソンメナーとジュドソンパークに16年間レジデントだった時に始まりました。
　彼女が亡くなった後、私はボランティアとして買い物を手伝ったり、訪問したりして他のレジデントと交流していました。
　4年前、私たちの素晴らしい過去の思い出と未来への対応を考えたとき、私の夫と私はジュドソンパークを我が家と呼ぶべき時が来たという決心をすることになりました。

　ジュドソンのライフスタイルに適応するのに時間はかかりませんでした。私たちは、多くの人々によって行われている、私たちを快適で幸せにしてくれるための努力に大変強い印象を受けました。そのことは今も変わりません。
　私たちはシンシア・ダン会長兼CEO（最高経営責任者）が立ち止まって、私たちの生活がどのように続けられているかや、多くのスタッフの1人が手のかかる問題解決にいつ取り組むのかについて話してくれた時にそのことを感じました。
　そして最後に、近くを散歩していた時に、長い間考えなければならないとは思っていましたが突き詰めて考えることがなかったことについて深く考え、将来への展望が開ける経験をしました。

　私たちがここに来る前は、歩くことは主に運動のためであり、他の雑用の合間にするだけのものでした。
　現在では、散歩は私の人生の歩みの中で生ずるいろいろな問題を乗り越えるのを助けてくれるものであるだけでなく、私が立ち止まって周りの景色を楽しみ、深毛の犬と仲良くしたり、鳥のさえず

the tree deflects harsh winter winds and gives respite from summer sun, Judson provides a buffer and solutions to the challenges that accompany aging. What a comfortable way to live during this phase of life. Thank you, Judson, and Happy Birthday!

—Josephine Rich

りに耳を傾け、そよ風に感動する時間を与えてくれるものとなりました。
　注目してもらうことを待っている美しいものを鑑賞することは何と贅沢なことでしょう。
　庭の1本の古木のそばに座り、私はその木を私たちの100歳になった（ジュドソンという）コミュニティになぞらえている自分に気がつきました。
　その木が厳しい冬の風をさえぎり、私たちを夏の太陽から守って休息を与えてくれるように、ジュドソンは加齢に伴うチャレンジを和らげ、解決策をもたらしてくれます。
　人生の後半を生きるのになんと快適な道でしょう。
　ジュドソン、ありがとう。お誕生日おめでとう。

　ジョセフィーン・リッチ

Part Two: Judson at University Circle 1906–2006 A Century of Excellence

2. INTRODUCTION

Tradition. When you think of Judson you think of state-of-the-art care, quality programming, longevity and an urbane, sophisticated atmosphere. But if you think of Judson as strictly bricks and mortar and services, you'll miss the biggest tradition of all—people.

Throughout its 100-year history, Judson has been guided by and has served an amazing, dynamic cadre of people who have discovered that aging is something to celebrate.

Here are their stories...

第2部 ユニバーシティサークルにおけるジュドソン 1906—2006 卓越の一世紀

2 前置き

　伝統。ジュドソンのことを考えるとき、あなたは最高水準のケア、質の高いプログラム、長寿、そして上品で洗練された雰囲気を思い浮かべるでしょう。しかしもしあなたが、ジュドソンのことを厳密に煉瓦や漆喰でできた施設の建物や、そこでのサービスで考えているなら、あなたはジュドソンの他の何にも増して大きな伝統、すなわち「人々」を見逃しています。

　100年の歴史を通して、ジュドソンは歳を重ねることは祝福すべき何かであると気づいたすばらしくダイナミックな一群の人々によって率いられ、またその人たちに奉仕してきました。

　ここから彼らの物語が始まります。

Part Two: Judson at University Circle 1906–2006 A Century of Excellence

3. It was Cleveland's Gilded Age...

(1) ... when Italianate mansions lined Euclid Avenue and the city's early industrialists, fresh from celebrating the city's centennial, embarked on massive charitable endeavors that would eventually lead to University Circle and Rockefeller Park.

But just down Euclid Avenue at the Euclid Avenue Baptist Church, the Women's Social Bible class met to discuss one Mrs. Sarah T. Garlock. She was elderly and ill and had no family, home or financial resources. She had been hospitalized at Deaconess and the women wondered how they could care for her.

She needed a home and looking after, and at her age she was not the only woman in need of such care. The women mobilized a capital campaign and one of the church's own, John D. Rockefeller, stepped forward and gave them $5,000 toward the purchase of a home at 3334 Prospect Avenue. It became known as the Baptist Home of Northern Ohio. Its mission: "to accommodate the aged of whom half a score have found it as restful as the 'shadow of a great rock in a weary land.'"

The six women who lived there had a home with a "contented and congenial atmosphere" for the remainder of their lives. Recognizing the need for caring for the elderly, the women of Euclid Avenue Baptist Church were joined by churches of other denominations, donating money, furniture

第2部 ユニバーシティサークルにおけるジュドソン 1906―2006 卓越の一世紀

3 それはクリーブランドの
　金色に輝く時代

(1)　…　イタリア風の邸宅がユークリッド通りに並び、初期の実業家たちが市の 100 年祭を祝ったばかりで、最後にはユニバーシティサークルやロックフェラー公園を生み出すことになる膨大な社会貢献事業への努力をはじめたとき

　クリーブランドのユークリッド通りを下ったところにあるユークリッド通りバプテスト教会の女性社会聖書教室に、ミセス・サラ・T・ガーロックという女性について話し合うために人々が集まった。
　彼女は高齢で病気であり家族も家庭も経済的たくわえもなかった。彼女はデアコネスにある病院に入院していたが、女性たちは彼女をどのようにお世話できるかいろいろと考えた。
　彼女には住むところと世話が必要だった。そして彼女の年齢ではそのようなケアを必要としているのは彼女だけではなかった。
　女性たちが募金のキャンペーンを組織したところ、教会の信者の1人であるジョン・D・ロックフェラー氏が歩み出て、プロスペクト通り3334番地の家を購入するため5,000ドルの寄付を申し出た。その家は北オハイオバプテストホームとして知られるようになった。そのホームの使命は、人々を疲れさせうんざりさせる荒地にある大きな岩の影のように、10人もの高齢者に安らかに休息できる場所を提供することであった。
　そこに住んだ6人の女性たちは満足し、気心の合った雰囲気の中で残りの人生を過ごした。

　高齢者をお世話することの大切さが認識されたため、ユークリッド通りバプテスト教会の女性たちに、他の宗派の教会の人々がお

クリーブランドの実業家 ジョン・D・ロックフェラー
Cleveland industrialist, John D. Rockefeller.

and provisions.

Before long the need for services outgrew the brick Victorian home and so in 1919 the ladies moved to a home at 8903 Cedar Avenue. That home provided 27 women with a place to live.

Also in 1919, just up Cedar Hill from the Baptist Home, Warren Bicknell, president of Cleveland Construction, was building his dream home—a reproduction 17th-century Jacobean English manor house—in the neighborhood known as Ambler Heights. The house was impressive, with 18 fireplaces, a massive oak door with wooden carvings, a secret passage to the wine cellar and a ballroom on the third floor.

第2部 ユニバーシティサークルにおけるジュドソン 1906—2006 卓越の一世紀

プロスペクト通りにあった北オハイオバプティストホーム
The Baptist Home of Northern Ohio on Prospect Avenue.

金や家具や食糧をもって加わった。

　やがてサービスの必要から、煉瓦造のビクトリア朝風の家では間に合わなくなり、1919年に女性たちはシーダー通り8903番地のホームに移った。そのホームは27人の女性の住み家となった。

　1919年のことだが、バプティストホームからシーダーヒルをちょうど上ったところに、クリーブランド建設社長のウオーレンビックネル氏が、17世紀の英国王ジェームズⅠ世時代風の邸宅で、近隣ではアンブラーハイツとして知られることとなった夢のホームともいえる家を建てていた。

　その家には18の暖炉や木製の彫刻がある大きなオークのドアがあり、また地下のワイン庫への秘密の通路や3階の舞踏場もあって目立つ建物だった。

　その家は40万ドルの建築費がかかっており、そこにはセントラルパークの景観を設計した建築士フレデリックオルムステッド氏によりデザインされた周囲より低い庭園があった。

It cost him $400,000 to build and included a sunken garden designed by Central Park landscape architect, Frederick Olmsted.

The brick and sandstone gabled Tudor was home to spectacular garden parties attended by Cleveland's elite, many of whom lived in the neighborhood. It was a fitting lifestyle for the man whose company built Cleveland Public Library and the Palace Theater. By 1939, the Baptist Home on Cedar was becoming crowded and unlivable. After its heyday, the Bicknell Mansion was on the market.

For a paltry $50,000, the Baptist Home of Northern Ohio became the owners of the opulent home, turning the former master suite and the third-floor ballroom into apartments.

Situated on seven acres atop the bluff on Cedar Hill, the Bicknell Mansion gave the Baptist Home plenty of space for its women and for future expansion. It was renamed the Baptist Home of Ohio in 1941 and eventually saw the additions of Mouat and Milner Hall in 1950 and 1951. The 10-story Jordan Gardner apartments were dedicated in 1974 and the entire community was renamed Judson Park in honor of Adoniram Judson, an American Baptist missionary working in Burma from 1812–1850.

(2) Throughout its history, Judson has been at the forefront of providing smart living choices for Clevelanders as they age, reinforcing the importance of physical exercise, cognitive stimulation and social engagement. From its inception, Judson has given individuals a choice about how to live their lives.

The Day Enrichment Center was added in 1977. Judson

第2部 ユニバーシティサークルにおけるジュドソン 1906—2006 卓越の一世紀

　煉瓦と砂岩の切り妻のある英国チューダー様式の建物は、近隣に住むクリーブランドのエリートたちが出席する華やかなガーデンパーティに使われる建物となっていた。自分の所有する建設会社がクリーブランド公立図書館とパレス劇場を建てたビックネル氏にとって、自己のライフスタイルに合致したものであった。
　1939年までにシーダーのバプティストホームは手狭になったため、住むのに適さなくなった。
　全盛時代の後、ビックネルの邸宅は売りに出された。
　ほんの5万ドルで北オハイオバプティストホームはビックネルの華やかな邸宅を手に入れ、前所有者の続きの間と3階の舞踏場をアパートに変えた。

　シーダーヒルの絶壁の頂上にある7エーカーの土地に建てられていたので、ビックネルの邸宅は女性たちのため、またバプティストホームが将来ホームを拡張するための広いスペースをそなえていた。
　この建物は1941年にオハイオバプティストホームと名を変えられ、やがて1950年と51年に建物としてムアト及びミルナーホールが付け加えられた。
　10階建てのジョーダンガードナーアパートメントが1974年に献納され、全体のコミュニティは1812年から1850年にビルマ（現ミャンマー）でアメリカンバプティスト宣教師として働いたアドニラム・ジュドソンを讃えてジュドソンパークと改名された。

(2)　ジュドソンは、その歴史を通してクリーブランドの人々に身体運動、知的刺激、社会との関わりの重要性を重視することにより、年齢に応じた「スマートリビング」の選択ができるよう、その先頭に立ってきた。
　当初からジュドソンは個人がどのように生きるかについての選択を自分で決定できるよう配慮してきた
　デイエンリッチメントセンター（デイサービスセンター）が1977

ウェードパークメナー（後のジュドソンメナー）
The Wade Park Manor (Later Judson Manor).

maintained a host of programming and health and wellness services for its independent and skilled nursing residents.

But the leadership was always looking for ways to improve services and expand choices for its residents.

Down the hill at E. 107th and Chester Avenue, the Wade Park Manor opened as a luxury residential hotel in 1923. It catered to Severance Hall musicians, business and political leaders and celebrities visiting Cleveland. Guests included Dwight D. Eisenhower, Walt Disney and Jack Benny.

After years of hosting Cleveland's upper crust, the Christian Residences Foundation, a nonprofit nonsectarian community organization comprised of seven area churches, purchased Wade Park Manor in 1964.

By 1983, the Christian Residences Foundation was

第2部 ユニバーシティサークルにおけるジュドソン 1906—2006 卓越の一世紀

年に開設された。自立棟や重介護棟のレジデントのためにたくさんのプログラムや健康維持のためのサービスが用意された。しかし組織のリーダーたちは利用者のためにさらにサービスを向上させ選択肢を増やすことを求めた。

チェスター通り東107番地に「ウエードパークメナー」が1923年に豪華な長期滞在型ホテルとしてオープンした。

そのホテルはセヴェランスホール（音楽堂）の音楽家、ビジネスや政治的リーダーのほかクリーブランドを訪れる有名人たちに料理のケータリングをした。ドワイト・アイゼンハワー大統領（当時）やウオルトディズニー、ジャックベニーもゲストに含まれていた。

クリーブランドの上流階級に利用された後に、非営利で7つの地域の教会からなるノンセクトのコミュニティ組織であるクリスチャン住宅財団が、1964年にウエードパークメナーを購入した。

1983年まで、クリスチャン住宅財団はメナーを客で満たそうと苦闘していた。かつて優美だったホテルも大修理を必要としていた。そこに住む人々も追加的なサービスを求めていた。

以前からジュドソンは、高齢者のための「スマートリビング」と同義語のように受け止められていた。理事会及び職員のリーダーシップと地域からの支援によって、ジュドソンはメナーのオーナーとなることを引き受けた。そしてすぐに（長期滞在者のためのアパートとして使用されていた）メナーのアパートの住人のためにキチンを付け加え、その他改修を行うための資金集めを始めた。

5週間足らずの間に、ジュドソンはこの計画のために90万ドルを集めた。日刊紙「ザ・プレインディーラー」は社説で次のように書いた。

「ジュドソンのこの訴えかけに対する模範的な近隣コミュニティの応答によって、ジュドソンとメナーそれぞれが持つ誇るべき伝統を継続するのに貢献するだろう」

メナーを獲得したことによりジュドソンは、自己を特徴づけるものとして、自立高齢者と重度の高齢者の中間にある人々のニーズを満たす機会を得ることになった。

struggling to fill the Manor. The once-elegant hotel was in dire need of renovation. And its residents were in need of some additional services.

Judson had long since become synonymous with smart living for older adults. Through the leadership of the board and staff and the support of the community, Judson assumed ownership of the Manor. It quickly launched a capital campaign to fund the addition of kitchens to the apartments and other renovations.

Within five short weeks, Judson had managed to raise $900,000 to support its efforts. In an editorial at the time *The Plain Dealer* wrote: "The exemplary community response to the institution's appeals will help continue two proud traditions."

Acquiring the Manor gave Judson the opportunity to fill a need it had identified for those residents who fell in between independent living and skilled nursing care. When the Manor was renovated, Judson became an early pioneer by dedicating two floors to residents requiring assisted living. And with the addition of the Manor, the organization became known as Judson Retirement Community.

In the mid-1970s, the late Ruth Wismar pioneered the concept of health maintenance, fostering an environment and a philosophy in which Judson was not going to wait until its residents were candidates for skilled care before becoming concerned with their health. Rather, it sought proactive ways to encourage maintenance of health and exercise, preventive interventions and early detection and successful management of chronic conditions.

第2部 ユニバーシティサークルにおけるジュドソン 1906—2006 卓越の一世紀

　メナーが改修されたとき、2つの階を支援を必要とするレジデント用に変えることによって、この分野の早期のパイオニアとなった。またメナーを加えることによって、組織はジュドソン・リタイアメント・コミュニティ(ジュドソン退職者共同体)として知られるようになった。
　70年代の半ばに、故ルース・ウスマールが、健康維持に関するコンセプトを開拓した。それは、利用者が自分の健康に気をつけなければならないと感じ始める以前に、利用者が重度化する前にジュドソンが行動を起こせるよう、環境と考え方（哲学）を変えていくよう促すものであった。この考えは、より正確には、健康維持と運動、予防的介入と早期発見、それに慢性状態の効果的管理を奨励する積極的傾向をもった方法を模索するものであった。

(3) By addressing the aging process in its entirety, Judson was able to provide its residents with a continuum of services that gave them the choice to live as independently as possible for as long as possible. Through its emphasis on extra support and understanding how to manage chronic conditions, Judson has helped many residents avoid a premature move to skilled nursing care.

In the early 1980s, Judson began realizing a continuum "without walls" when it took on its first home care case with the Bruening family.

Word spread about the quality of in-home care Judson could provide, and by the 1990s the organization founded Judson Home Care.

As medical professionals began to better understand the brain's function as one ages, Judson professionals turned that knowledge into new and better ways of caring for those residents through its memory support program.

Skilled nursing care was also changing and by 1991, Judson opened the state-of-the-art Bruening Health Center, which set a new standard for skilled care. The addition of a pool allowed Judson to open its doors wider to the community.

With Bruening, Judson completed its continuum and by 1994 it was named one of the best Continuing Care Retirement Communities (CCRC) in America by *New Choices for Retirement Living*.

Judson continually enhances and refines its programs and services. In 1999, it became the first site in Northeast Ohio to embrace the Eden Alternative, a strategy for acknowledging the important relationships between staff and residents. Judson fashioned its own "brand of Eden," engaging staff at all levels and all departments toward Judson's mission.

第2部 ユニバーシティサークルにおけるジュドソン 1906—2006 卓越の一世紀

(3) 人が年齢を重ねていく過程に全体として対応することにより、ジュドソンはレジデントにできるだけ長くできる限り自立して生きる選択ができるようにするための（体力・健康の程度に応じて変化対応できる）連続的なサービスを提供することが可能になった。（「連続的」の意味は「継続的」の意味とは峻別して使われている―編者注）慢性症状にどのように対応するかについての特別の支援と理解を強調することを通して、ジュドソンは多くのレジデントが重介護棟へ早期に移動しなければならなくなることを避ける手助けをした。

1980年代初頭、ブリューニング家の家族と協力してホームケアの最初のケースに手を染めた時、自宅において断絶のない連続的サービスを提供する最初の試みを始めた。

ジュドソンが提供する自宅でのケアの質の高さについての評判が広まり、1990年代までに組織はジュドソンホームケア事業を立ち上げた。

医療の専門家が加齢に伴う脳の機能変化への理解を深めるに従って、ジュドソンの専門家は利用者の記憶サポートプログラムを通してケアするという新たなより優れた方法へ舵を切った。

重度者への介護の方法にも変化があり、1991年までにジュドソンは重度者対応の最高水準のブリューニングヘルスセンターを設置した。そこで重介護に関する新しい基準を定めた。またプールの設置によってジュドソンは地域社会とより広いつながりを持つことになった。

ブリューニングヘルスセンターを設置することによってジュドソンは、高齢化のそれぞれの段階に応じて高齢者の必要に応えることのできる連続的ケアの体制を完成した。

そしてその結果、1994年までに雑誌「ニューチョイスイズ・フォー・リタイアメントリビング」により全米で最優秀の継続的ケア退職者コミュニティの1つであると命名された。

ジュドソンは、休むことなくプログラムとサービスの向上に努め、磨きをかけ続けてきている。

The result has been a growing network of community collaborations including curriculum-driven partnerships with local schools. These groups bring over 500 youngsters monthly through Judson's doors. Residents also participate in an array of programs at schools and with civic groups that give them the opportunity to volunteer with and to mentor young people.

Recognizing Judson's culture of engagement and inclusiveness, the Cleveland-based Employer Resource Council bestowed its NorthCoast 99 Award, honoring Judson as one of the "99 Best Places to Work in Northeast Ohio."

Throughout its 100 years, Judson at University Circle has embraced this kind of forward thinking and compassion, offering smart choices for its residents. As it continues to forge an ever-widening network of community partnerships—something that Judson has nurtured from its very beginning.

第2部 ユニバーシティサークルにおけるジュドソン 1906—2006 卓越の一世紀

　1999年にスタッフとレジデント間の関係の重要性を認識するための戦略である「エデン・オールターナティブ（エデンの園に代わるものを意味する）」を取り込み採用した北東オハイオ地域での最初の施設となった。
　すべてのレベル、すべての分野のスタッフをジュドソンの使命に引き込んで、ジュドソンは自己独自のエデンブランドを創り上げた。
　その結果、地域の学校とのカリキュラムに組み入れられた協力関係を含む地域社会との協力によって、地域に広がっていくネットワークが出来上がった。これらのグループは毎月500人以上の若者をジュドソンの門に招き入れた。レジデントも一連の学校でのプログラムに市民グループとともに参加し、そのことが彼らにとって一緒にボランティア活動をしたり若者に助言したりする機会となっている。
　職員の雇用の確保と組織に関係するすべての人々を包み込むジュドソンの組織文化を評価し、クリーブランドに本拠を置く「雇用者資源会議（エンプロイヤー・リソース・カウンシル）」は、ジュドソンを北東オハイオにおける99の最優秀事業所の1つとして表彰した。
　100年の歴史を通して、ユニバーシティサークルにあるジュドソンは、前進しようとする考えと情熱をもってレジデントのためのスマートリビングを提供してきた。創設時からはぐくんできたもの、すなわちますます広がるコミュニティとのパートナーシップのネットワークをジュドソンは発展させ続けている。

Part Two: Judson at University Circle 1906–2006 A Century of Excellence

4. COMMUNITY PARTNER AND RESOURCE

(1) When it first opened in 1906, Judson was an outreach of the Euclid Avenue Baptist Church. But it also relied on the generosity and partnerships of other nearby congregations.

Today it is clear that Judson's boundaries are permeable. It continues to find and nurture those partnerships that help people make smart living choices.

Physical activity is a key component to maintaining a healthy lifestyle. Sara Peckham, director of wellness and resident life since 1992, developed the health and wellness philosophy that brings a wealth of programs to both residents

第2部 ユニバーシティサークルにおけるジュドソン 1906—2006 卓越の一世紀

4 コミュニティパートナーと
　地域の資源としてのジュドソン

(1)　ジュドソンが1906年に最初に開設されたとき、その事業はユークリッド通りバプティスト教会から始まった事業だった。しかしそれはまた、他の近隣の集まりの寛容とパートナーシップ（協力関係）にも支えられていた。今日ではジュドソンの活動は社会に柔軟に浸透している。

　ジュドソンは、人々が「スマートリビング」を選ぶのに役立つ近隣とのパートナーシップを見つけ出し、育て続けている。

　身体運動は健康的なライフスタイルを維持するための鍵となる構成要素である。
　1992年以来、ジュドソンのウエルネス・利用者生活担当部長のサラ・ペッカムは、広域クリーブランドをカバーする革新的なジュドソンの活動拠点において、レジデントと何千という参加メンバーの双方に有益なプログラムを提供する健康に関するフィロソフィーを発展させてきた。
　「ジュドソンは地域社会の資源です。私たちはすべて歳をとっていきます。70歳代、80歳代に達するにつれて弱っていく体力のように、私たちが直面するそれぞれの人生の時期における問題があります。
　もしあなたが元気を失ったり、歩くことも起き上がることも坐ることもできなければ、世間から隠遁することは簡単にできます。スタッフと私は、人々に強く生き続けるよう援助するための健康教育プログラムと活動計画を発展させてきました」とペッカム部長は言う。
　すべての年齢に適合できる温水プールと運動プログラムを利用することにより、ジュドソンは地域社会にとって健康を享受するための評判の場所となった。時に地域の人々はお互い同士交流した後リ

and thousands of members and participants at innovative community satellite sites throughout Greater Cleveland.

"Judson is a community resource," she explains. "We're all aging, but there are certain lifespan issues we all face, such as decreased strength, as we reach our seventh and eighth decade. If you feel no energy or can't walk or get up and sit down, it's easy to withdraw from the world. My staff and I have developed health education programs and action plans to help people stay strong," says Ms. Peckham.

With the use of the warm-water pool and exercise programs tailored to all ages, Judson is a popular place for the community to enjoy wellness. Sometimes they come for outpatient rehabilitation after joint replacement. Other times they come to visit a friend or relative. But they keep coming back to partake of the community's wellness offerings. "You can continue to come here even if you never choose to live here," says Ms. Peckham.

She is always looking at ways to maximize collaborations with others to expand Judson's range of services. The Arthritis Foundation provides programs in which trainers help people with warm-water exercises in the pool.

Children from nearby communities come to Judson for swim lessons and love the warm water.

Judson offers aerobics, stretching, Pilates, yoga and tai chi. "Wellness isn't just physical," says Ms. Peckham, "it's also emotional, spiritual, psychological and cultural. We help people stay engaged by using the skills they already have and encouraging them to be active."

Those relationships extend to the broader community. For years, Judson has worked with Cleveland, Cleveland Heights and Shaker Heights to develop and offer programs

第2部 ユニバーシティサークルにおけるジュドソン 1906—2006 卓越の一世紀

ハビリ外来にやって来る。また友人や親戚に会いに来る。しかし彼らはコミュニティが健康維持のために提供するものを共に享受するために必ず戻ってくる。

ペッカム部長は、それらの人々に「あなた方がここに入居することを選ばなくても、ずっとこれからも来てください」という。

彼女は常にジュドソンのサービス提供の範囲を拡げるため、他の人々との協力を最大にするための方法を考えている。

関節炎財団はジュドソンのプールでトレーナーが人々に温水運動の手助けをするためのプログラムを提供してくれている。近隣の子供たちは水泳教室に来て温水と親しんでいる。

ジュドソンでは、エアロビクス・ストレッチ体操・ピラテス・ヨガ・太極拳などを行っている。

「健康は身体的なものだけではありません。それはまた、情緒的・精神的・心理的・文化的側面を持っています。私たちはそれぞれが持っているスキルを生かして、アクティブに生きていけるよう力づけることによって、人々が社会とのつながりを保ち続けられるよう援助していきます」とペッカム部長は言う。

これらの関係は、より広いコミュニティに拡げられていく。何年もの間、ジュドソンはクリーブランド・クリーブランドハイツ・シェーカーハイツ（それぞれ隣接する市である：編者注）と協力してシニアのためのプログラムを発展させ、提供するために働いてきた。

「2005年に150人以上のシェーカーハイツ市民がジュドソンの水中運動や健康プログラムに参加しました。ジュドソンがシェーカーハイツ市とユニバーシティサークルに隣接しているため家族や友人が訪問しやすいだけでなく、その上生活の状態が変わった時も、終わることなく人々が生涯学習を続けるための、人生を豊かにしエキサイティングなものとする環境をジュドソンは用意してくれているのです」とシェーカーハイツのジューディス・H・ローソン市長は言う。

and services for seniors.

"In 2005, more than 150 Shaker Heights residents have enjoyed the aquatic exercise and wellness programs," says Mayor Judith H. Rawson of Shaker Heights. "Judson's proximity to Shaker Heights and to University Circle not only makes it easy for family and friends to visit, but provides an enriching and exciting environment for lifetime learning that doesn't end when living arrangements change."

(2) Recognizing that people want to stay in their homes longer, Judson has started a new initiative which provides the community with services such as handyman, lawn maintenance and housekeeping to ease the challenges of home maintenance.

True to its promise to work with the communities it serves, Judson explored with the cities of Cleveland, Cleveland Heights and Shaker Heights à la carte services that give residents the option of staying in their homes longer.

Members in the greater community work with a coordinator to help schedule anything from a workout and lunch at Café Louise to having their gutters cleaned.

This extended membership program creates a virtual retirement community that provides resources for those who choose to live in their homes. Regardless, Judson wants people to know that it is a resource for all.

Kay Coss retired early from Cleveland Heights-University Heights Schools. A resident of Cleveland Heights, she turned to Judson after her doctor told her she needed to

第2部 ユニバーシティサークルにおけるジュドソン 1906—2006 卓越の一世紀

サラ・ペッカム ウェルネス担当部長
Sara Peckham, Judson Wellness Director.

（2）　人々が自宅でできる限り長く生活したいと望んでいることが明白なので、自宅での生活を容易にするため、ジュドソンは便利屋（よろずや）、芝刈りやハウスキーパーのようなサービスを地域社会に提供するための新しい試みを始めた。

　地域社会とともに働くという約束にたがわず、ジュドソンはクリーブランド市・クリーブランドハイツ市・シェーカーハイツ市とともに、住民にできる限り長く自宅で生活を続けるという選択ができるようにするためのアラカルトサービスを考えた。

　（ジュドソンの組織につながる人々全体の）大コミュニティのメンバーは、コーディネーターと協力して身体運動や「カフェルイーズ」でのランチから屋根の樋の掃除まで、なんでも手伝いをするためのスケジュールを立てる手助けをするために働いている。

　この拡大された会員プログラムは、自宅での生活を続けることを選んだ人々のために必要な資源を供給する事実上の退職者コミュニティを作り上げている。

　ジュドソンはすべての人々にとって利用できる地域の「資源」であることを人々に知ってもらいたいと望んでいる。

　ケイ・コスはクリーブランド市とユニバーシティハイツ市の学校を早期退職した。クリーブランドハイツ市の市民である彼女は、

lower her blood pressure. "He gave me six months to try diet and exercise before putting me on medications," she says.

So she went with a friend to the water aerobics class. "I knew I lacked the discipline to do this at home," says Ms. Coss. "At Judson, the water is 90 degrees and no one judges you."

With diet and exercise she lowered her blood pressure to what it was when she was in her 20s and she lost 40 pounds. "I've always been fairly active, but I've gotten a lot stronger than I used to be. I have a lot more energy now."

So strong that she has no trouble maintaining her Japanese garden or moving bricks to reset her brick driveway.

She's also taken weight classes led by Judson staff at the Cleveland Heights Recreation Center. "It's really also become a social event because we laugh and have a lot of fun. Judson keeps me moving," she says.

Partnerships elevate the choices available to all, whether people want to come to Judson for special programs or whether residents want to go into the community to continue their volunteer activities.

At the suggestion of a staff member, Judson has hosted Girl Scout overnights connected with the Swim for Diabetes. The girls swim for the charity event in the Judson pool and the next morning host a pancake breakfast to raise more money for the Diabetes Association of Greater Cleveland.

Other partnerships include residents who head out into the community to serve as reading tutors to local schoolchildren and as surrogate grandparents to local children whose own grandparents don't live nearby.

かかりつけ医が血圧を下げることが必要であると彼女に告げた後、ジュドソンに行った。
「彼は私に、薬物療法を受ける前に6か月間のダイエットと運動療法を行う猶予を与えてくれました」と彼女は言う。
　そこで彼女はウオーターエアロビクスに友達と一緒に行った。
「私はこれを自宅で行える訓練ができていないことを知っています。ジュドソンでは水温は90度（華氏）となっており、だれもエアロビクスの結果についてとやかく言いません」
　ダイエットと運動をすることにより彼女は血圧を20代のときの水準にまで下げ、40ポンド（約18キロ）体重を下げた。
「私はいつもかなり積極的な性格でしたが、以前より大いに強くなりました。私は今では以前より大変エネルギッシュになっています」
　彼女は自宅の日本庭園の世話をしたり、自宅の煉瓦を敷きつめた自動車用の道を整備するために煉瓦を並べ直すことができるまでになった。彼女はクリーブランドハイツリクリエーションセンターでジュドソンのスタッフが指導しているウエイトクラスに参加した。
「私たちは笑い、大変楽しいので、そこは実際楽しい社交の場となっています。ジュドソンは私を活発に活動させてくれます」
　人々がジュドソンに特別のプログラムのために来たいと思おうが、レジデントがボランティア活動を続けるためにコミュニティに出て行きたいと思おうが、どちらであってもジュドソンと地域社会との協力関係は人々の選択肢を広げてくれている。
　ジュドソンのスタッフの提案で、「糖尿病のための水泳」のためにジュドソンは夜通しガールスカウトの活動のホスト役を務めた。少女たちはジュドソンのプールでチャリティ事業の催しのために泳ぎ、そして次の朝には広域クリーブランド地域の糖尿病協会のための募金活動としてパンケーキの朝食会のホスト役をつとめた。
　地域とのその他の協力については、ジュドソンのレジデントが地域の子供たちに読書を教えるボランティアをしたり、祖父母が近くに住んでいない地域の子供たちに祖父母の代わりをつとめるボランティアをしたりしている。

5. THE HEART AND SOUL

(1) There is a feeling of warmth that envelops you when you first enter Judson. It's genuine and heartfelt. It's there because of the people who choose to live at Judson and those who choose to work there.

Marge Townsend knows more than the average resident about Judson. Her husband, Norman, was the long-time executive director, overseeing it through the acquisition of Judson Manor and the construction of Bruening Health Center. Since he and his wife had a farm in Ashtabula County, Mr. Townsend also maintained a tiny apartment in the Bicknell Mansion.

"Norm loved being here and he loved the people. He kept an apartment upstairs in the mansion so he wouldn't have to make the long commute home every night," she says.

Mr. Townsend retired in 1992. Sadly, he was diagnosed with brain cancer and died two years later. Ms. Townsend came to Judson Manor in 2000. Though she looked at other places, she found Judson Manor had the best array of services. "My newspaper is right outside my door (and it's dry). I make my own coffee and breakfast. I'm taking organ lessons at the Cleveland Music School Settlement," she says. She enjoys the exercise room, particularly the weights and stationary bike, and has an embroidery machine and computer.

An alumna of Case Western Reserve University, she receives e-mails about university events and enjoys walking the campus and seeing the young people. She also enjoys patronizing the Cleveland Orchestra, the Cleveland Play House and the Cleveland Opera.

第2部 ユニバーシティサークルにおけるジュドソン 1906—2006 卓越の一世紀

5 心と魂

(1) あなた方がジュドソンに入ったとき、温かい雰囲気を感じるだろう。それは偽りのない心からのものである。なぜならジュドソンで生活することを選び、またそこで働くことを選んだ人々がそこにいることがその理由である。

マージ・タウンセンドはジュドソンについて平均的レジデントより詳しく知っている。彼女の夫のノーマンはジュドソンがジュドソンメナーを取得した時やブリューニングヘルスセンターを建設した時にジュドソンの監督責任を担った、長年にわたる執行役員だったからだ。

タウンセンド氏と彼の妻がアシュタブラ県に農場を持っていたので、彼はジュドソンパークにあるビックネルマンションの中に小さなアパートを借りた。

「ノーマンはそこにいることが好きで、またそこにいる人々が好きでした。彼はマンションの2階にアパートを借りたので、毎夜自宅へ帰るための通勤に長く時間をかける必要がありませんでした」とマージは言う。

タウンセンド氏は1992年にリタイアした。悲しいことに脳のがんと診断され、2年後に亡くなった。

タウンセンド夫人は2000年にジュドソンメナーに入居した。彼女は他の場所も見てきたが、メナーには最良のサービスがあると知った。

「私の新聞は、私の部屋のドアの前に（ぬれずに）置かれています。私は自分のコーヒーと朝食を作ります。私はオルガンのレッスンをクリーブランド音楽学校セツルメントで受けています」

彼女は運動部屋でウエートトレーニングと静止バイクによる運動をし、刺繍用のミシンとコンピュータを使う。

ケース・ウエスタンリザーブ大学の卒業生で、大学からイベントに関するメールをもらう。キャンパスを歩き、若者と出会うことを

"It's a very secure feeling living in a continuing care retirement community," she says, especially now that her daughter runs the family farm. "It's a safety net for me and for my daughter," she says.

Under his leadership, the first time that someone other than a Baptist minister ran the community, Mr. Townsend sought to expand services. He brought in adult day care and embarked on major building efforts, particularly the $28.5 million Bruening Health Center. "It was risky because there was a lot of money involved. But Norm felt very strongly that people should be able to live here and visit their spouse if the spouse required more extensive care."

"Norm's legacy at Judson is the special way he cared for people. Even today, there is still that sense of caring," she says.

(2) Allen Ford is grateful for Norman Townsend's efforts in establishing the Bruening Health Center. He and his late wife Connie moved to the Manor a few years ago.

Mr. Ford was able to visit Connie daily in Bruening while still keeping a busy schedule of activities. He describes himself as a "member of the old economy." He was in iron ore and mining and was chief financial officer of Sohio before BP took it over. And he's been active all around University Circle, serving on boards at the Cleveland Orchestra, University Circle Inc., Western Reserve Historical Society, Case Western Reserve University and University Hospitals.

第2部 ユニバーシティサークルにおけるジュドソン 1906—2006 卓越の一世紀

楽しむ。
　彼女はまたクリーブランドオーケストラやクリーブランド劇場、クリーブランドオペラの後援者であることに喜びを見出している。「継続的ケアの退職者コミュニティの生活は大変安全で安心できる気持ちにさせてくれます」と、今では家族の農場の経営を娘が引き受けてくれていることもあって、そのように言う。
「私と私の娘にとってジュドソンで生活することはセーフティネットなのです」
　バプティスト派の聖職者以外がジュドソンの経営を引き受けることになったのはタウンセンド氏のリーダーシップの下で初めて実現したが、彼はサービスの幅を拡げようとした。彼は成人を対象とするデイサービスを導入し、主要な建設計画への努力、特に2,850万ドルをかけたブリューニングヘルスセンター建設に着手した。
「それは多額のお金がかかるのでリスクを伴うものでした。しかし、彼はもし配偶者がより広いケアを必要とするなら、人々がジュドソンに住み、重度者の棟にいる自分の配偶者を訪ねることができるようにすべきだと強く感じていました。ジュドソンにノーマンが残したものは、人々をお世話する特別の方法です。ここには今でもケアの仕方に特別の気働き（センス）があります」と彼女は言う。

(2) 　アレン・フォードはノーマン・タウンセンドがブリューニングヘルスセンターを創設した努力に感謝している。
　彼と亡くなった妻のコニーはメナーに数年前に移ってきた。フォード氏はまだ仕事で忙しいスケジュールの中にいたが、ブリューニングにいるコニーを訪問することができた。
　彼は自分をオールドエコノミーのメンバーであると表現する。
　彼は鉄鉱石と鉱業の仕事に関わり、ブリティッシュペトロリアム社が経営権を取得するまではソヒオ社の最高財務担当役員であった。
　彼はユニバーシティサークル周辺一帯でクリーブランドオーケストラ、ユニバーシティサークル社、ウエスタンリザーブ歴史ソサイ

But he's hardly out of touch with the new. He and his wife endowed a professorship in biomedical engineering at Case. Not because that's what he did for a living, but because he is a forward-thinking businessman who has a great interest in the breakthroughs taking place between the fields of medicine and engineering.

That interest also led him to work on the launch of another University Circle gem, BioEnterprise, an organization devoted to growing bioscience companies in Northeast Ohio.

Mr. Ford, along with his brother, Dr. Amasa Ford, are honorary co-chairs of the Judson Centennial Celebration.

Mr. Ford's roots in University Circle are deep. His father, David Knight Ford, started The Abington Foundation, named for the New England town where his ancestors first settled. In fact, his family established a farm on what eventually became Case Western Reserve University and University Hospitals.

The Abington Foundation continues to support education, healthcare, economic self-sufficiency and cultural activities. Judson allows him to be near all the things that have been important to his family for decades

Robert and Barbara (Buster) Oldenburg live in what was once the master suite in the Bicknell Mansion. They met in Spanish class at Western Reserve and married in 1949. Throughout their lives, they have been proactive about the aging process.

Ms. Oldenburg has long been involved with organizations committed to successful aging, having served on boards or worked at Golden Age Centers, Benjamin Rose Institute, Access to the Arts and the Cleveland Heights Office on Aging.

It was important that they be able to live close to the

第2部 ユニバーシティサークルにおけるジュドソン 1906—2006 卓越の一世紀

エティ、ケース・ウエスタンリザーブ大学それに大学病院の役員会のメンバーとして活躍していた。

しかし彼は新しいものに疎くはなかった。

彼と彼の妻は（ウエスタンリザーブ大学との合併前の：編者注）ケース大学で生物医学エンジニアリングの教授の地位を与えられていた。生活のために何をしたかではなく、医学とエンジニアリングの分野間で起こるブレイクスルーに大きな興味を持つ進取的考えを持つビジネスマンであったからである。

彼の関心に従い、もう一つのユニバーシティサークルの宝ともいうべき生物エンタープライズすなわち北東オハイオの発展する生物科学の事業に乗り出す仕事に就いた。

フォード氏は彼の兄弟であるアマサ・フォード博士とともにジュドソン百年祭の共同名誉会長になった。

ユニバーシティサークルにおけるフォード氏のルーツは深い。彼の父のデイビッド・ナイト・フォード氏は、彼の先祖が最初に移住したニューイングランドの町の名にちなんだアービントン財団を創設した。

事実彼の家族は、今ではケース・ウエスタンリザーブ大学と大学病院があるところに農場を創った。

アービントン財団は教育・ヘルスケア・経済的自給自足や文化活動を支援し続けている。ジュドソンは何十年にもわたって彼の家族にとって重要だった場所の全てに彼らが自由に出入りすることを認めている。

ロバートとバーバラ・（バスター）・オルデンバーグは、ビックネルマンションの元の主人の続きの間（スイートルーム）であったところに住んでいる。彼らはウエスタンリザーブ大学（ケース大学と合併前の：編者注）のスペイン語クラスで会い、1949年に結婚した。彼らの人生を通して彼らはエイジング（歳を重ねること）について積極的に対応してきた。

オルデンバーグ夫人はサクセスフルエイジング（上手に歳をとっ

people and places they so enjoy such as the Cleveland Orchestra and University Circle's annual Parade the Circle event. "Judson's location was so important to us," she says. "We enjoy attending Orchestra concerts and volunteering out in the community."

Mr. Oldenburg can often be seen watering plants, fixing a fountain, or driving people to their appointments.

"It's nothing really, just gopher stuff," he says. But to the people he helps it means a great deal. And he's an ambassador for the continuing care retirement community concept. "It's so important to have this. We enjoy the friends and staff here and the proximity to our old friends," he says.

"We didn't want to be a burden to our children, who all live out of state," says Ms. Oldenburg. "We like having our independence here and found it wasn't that hard to give up our house."

第2部 ユニバーシティサークルにおけるジュドソン 1906—2006 卓越の一世紀

てゆくこと）に関わる組織と長い期間関係があり、ゴールデンエイジセンターズ、ベンジャミン・ローズ・インスティテュート、アクセス・トゥー・ジ・アートと「エイジングについてのクリーブランドハイツオフィス」の役員として、また職員として働いた。

クリーブランドオーケストラや、ユニバーシティサークルの毎年のイベントであるパレードのような楽しみを経験できる人や場所の近くに住むことができることが重要だった。

「ジュドソンがある場所は私たちにとって大変重要です。私たちはオーケストラのコンサートを聴きに行ったり、地域社会でボランティア活動を行ったりすることにより楽しい経験をしているのです」と彼女は言う。

オルデンバーグ氏が植物に水をやったり、噴水を整えたり、約束の場所に人を車で送って行ったりするのをしばしば見かけることができる。

「実際そんなことは何でもないことだ」と彼は言う。

しかし彼の助けを受ける人にとっては大変ありがたいことなのだ。そして彼は継続的退職者コミュニティのコンセプトにとっては大使とも言える人である。

「こういう仕事を持つことは大変重要なことなのだ。我々はここで友人や職員と楽しい時を過ごし、また古い友人の近くに居ることができるからだ」と彼は言う。

「子供たちは全員オハイオ州以外に住んでいますが、私たちは子供たちの重荷になりたくありません。私たちはここで独立して生活したいし、自分の家を持たないことはそれほど辛いことではありません」とオルデンバーグ夫人は言う。

(3) Dr. Joan Mortimer isn't about to slow down. She'll tell you that she's a very plan-ahead person and when she saw Judson Manor while looking for places to downsize she knew it was the right move for her and her late husband, Edward. An assistant professor Emerita of psychiatry at Case, the location in University Circle was key.

She laughs when she remembers the response of some of her friends wondering why she was 'going into' Judson and how she would stand an apartment. "First of all, I wasn't 'going into' anyplace, I was simply moving. I grew up outside New York City so I was accustomed to apartment living.

Though she and her husband owned two homes, she welcomed not having to arrange for snowplow service or pool maintenance. "I was aware from the beginning that it was a community of interesting people. I enjoy being involved and I like having the continuum as security," she says.

Living at the Manor allows her the freedom to pursue the things that are important to her, most of which happen at University Circle—helping youngsters to read at a nearby charter school, studying flute at the Cleveland Music School Settlement and auditing courses on subjects such as Hinduism at Case. But she also indulges in her favorite cultural activities, including the Cleveland Orchestra and The Cleveland Museum of Art.

"Education opens windows on the world and is invariably a cure for almost any ailment," she says. She doesn't simply indulge in education for herself, she also shares it with others. Along with a few other Manor residents, Dr. Mortimer is involved with an Internet publishing site, www.goldenark.org, which publishes mini-books online for children in various age groups.

第2部 ユニバーシティサークルにおけるジュドソン 1906—2006 卓越の一世紀

(3) ジョアン・モーティマー博士はスローダウンしているわけではない。彼女は自分が先回りして計画を立てる人間で、自分が生活をダウンサイズするための場所を探していたとき、ジュドソンメナーを見て彼女と亡夫のエドワードにとってそこが転居するのにいいところだと考えたと言うだろう。

ケース大学の精神医学の名誉准教授である彼女にとって、ユニバーシティサークルにあるというロケーションは決定的に重要であった。彼女の友達の何人かが彼女がなぜジュドソンに入ろうとするのか、またアパートで生活することにどのように耐えられるのかを心配して示した反応を思いだして笑う。

「まず第一に、私はどこにも入って行きません。私はただ移動するだけです。私はニューヨーク市の郊外で育ったので、アパートに住むことに慣れています」

彼女と彼女の夫は2軒の家を持っていたが、雪かきやプールの維持に気を使わなくてよいことを歓迎した。「私は最初からメナーが関心を持てる人々のコミュニティであることを知っていました。私はそこに住む人々の仲間になることを楽しみ、また連続的ケアが受けられる場所を安全のために求めました」

メナーで生活することは彼女にとって重要なことを追求できる自由を与えてくれる。そしてその大半はユニバーシティサークルで起こるものだ。近くのチャータースクール（公募型研究開発校）で読書をする若者の手助けをし、クリーブランド音楽学校セツルメントでフルートを習い、ケース・ウエスタンリザーブ大学でヒンドゥーイズムをテーマとするコースを聴講するようなことだ。

しかし彼女はまたクリーブランドオーケストラやクリーブランド美術館を含む好みの文化的活動にものめりこんでいる。

「教育は世界に対し窓を開け、ほとんどすべての慢性の病気にも常に治療薬の役割を果たします」と彼女は言う。

彼女は自分自身の教育にいつも浸っているだけでなく、他の人々とも分かち合う。

"You don't move to Judson and close the door behind you," she says. Rather it has opened doors to a vibrant life.

Helen Burdg is an expert at downsizing households for moves into independent and assisted living environments. She helped move more than 400 residents to Judson Park and Manor through her company, Smooth Moves. She would get to know the future resident and help them make decisions about furniture to keep and arrange in their new apartment.

So when the time came in 2002 for the Burdgs to downsize, they knew she would come to the Manor.

(4) "We're like family here."
—Libby Leggiero, Resident Life Assistant

"I see people vacillating and it's important for them to do this at a time when they can really enjoy it. You can be as independent or involved as you want to be. You can be alone or with people."

Ms. Burdg values her quiet time, but she's also found friends with the same likes and energy. "We giggle a lot here," she says.

他の何人かのメナーのレジデントとともに、モーティマー博士はインターネットでの出版サイトにかかわっている。（www.goldenark.org）それはオンラインでいろんな年齢のグループの子供たち向きのミニブックを発行している。

「あなた方はジュドソンに移ってきても外界と隔てる扉を背後で閉めてはいけません」と彼女は言う。ジュドソンに移ってきたことにより、かえって活気に満ちた人生への新しい扉が開かれることになる。

ヘレン・バードグは、ジュドソンの自立棟・要支援棟という環境に移動するに際して家族のサイズが小さくなることによって生ずる問題に対処するエキスパートだ。スムーズムーブという名の彼女の会社を通して400人以上のレジデントがジュドソンパークとメナーに転居してくるのを援助した。

彼女は将来ジュドソンのレジデントとなる人を知ってそれらの人たちが新しいアパートでどのような家具を揃え、整理すればいいのかを決める手助けをする。

2002年に今度はバードグ家の人々自身が一家をダウンサイズすべき時が来たと感じたとき、彼らは彼女がメナーに移ることを決めた。

(4) 私たちはここで家族のように暮らしています
レジデントライフアシスタント／リビー・レギエロ

「私は人々が自分がどうすればいいか迷っている姿を見ることがあります。しかし楽しめるときに楽しむことが大切です。私たちは一人で居たいときには一人で、人々とともに居たい時には人々とともにすごせばいいのです」

バードグさんは静かな時間に価値を置く。しかし彼女はまた、彼女と同じ好みを持ち同じように元気な人を見つけた。「私たちはここで一緒に笑ってばかり」と彼女はいう。

Access to the continuum of care was a big part of her decision. "I know I'll be cared for independent of my children. And being a nonprofit, I know I'll be able to stay if my money runs out," she says.

Her apartment is on the eighth floor of the Manor and overlooks Wade Lagoon and University Circle. It's so spectacular that it has inspired her to write poetry. "Judson feels very much a part of me. I keep active mentally and physically and that's so important to feeling healthy." An all-around enthusiast, Ms. Burdg serves on the executive committee of the Resident Council at the Manor. Her efforts include raising money for little improvements like new lampshades in the Manor common areas. But she also indulges her own passion for watercolor painting, exercise and gardening. She recently worked on installations at the Cleveland Botanical Garden.

Working at Judson gives staff members a front-row seat to see the changes in how people age.

"One of the biggest benefits of working here is seeing the different ways people age," says Libby Leggiero, Resident Life Assistant and Associate Director of Volunteer Services. "I see that the people who always have a good attitude toward life age well."

While Judson encourages and offers an active lifestyle, Ms. Leggiero says it's the people connections that are Judson's real gift. "We're like family here and we share both the good times and the bad," she says.

第2部 ユニバーシティサークルにおけるジュドソン 1906—2006 卓越の一世紀

　連続的ケアの施設と接触したのは彼女の大きな決心によるものであった。
「私はここが子供たちから独立してケアを受けることができるところであることを知っていました。非営利組織の経営なので、もし私のお金が不足したとしてもここに居ることができることも知っています」
　彼女のアパートはメナーの8階にある。そこからウエードラグーンやユニバーシティサークルが見渡せる。そこは見晴らしがよく、そのことが彼女に詩を作るよういざなう。
「ジュドソンはすっかり私の一部となりました。私は精神的・肉体的にアクティブであり続け、それは自分が健康であると感じるために大変重要なことなのです」
　オールラウンドの情熱家であるバードグさんは、メナーのレジデントカウンシル(レジデント協議会)の執行委員である。
　彼女の働きはメナーの共用エリアのランプの笠を新しくするような小さな改善のために募金活動をするようなことも含んでいる。
　しかし彼女はまた水彩画を描いたり運動やガーデニングをするなど、情熱の赴くままに熱中している。彼女は最近クリーブランド植物園の植物を整え世話することに取り組んでいる。

　ジュドソンで働くことは、人々がどのように齢をとっていくかの変化を見るのに、もっともよい最前の漕ぎ手の席をスタッフメンバーに与えてくれる。「ここで働いていて大変ありがたいと思うことは、人々の齢のとり方の違いを見ることができることです」とレジデントライフアシスタントでボランティアサービス部の提携部長であるリビー・レギエロはいう。
「私は人生に対していい態度をとっている人はうまく齢をとっていくことを見ています」
　彼女はジュドソンが積極的なライフスタイルを奨励し提供しているとしても、ジュドソンの本当の贈り物は人々とのつながりであるという。

113

Part Two: Judson at University Circle 1906–2006 A Century of Excellence

ジュドソンでは、すべてのレベルの職員に対して、
未来のリーダーになるためのトレーニングを行っている。

Judson fosters an environment where all levels of staff are encouraged to participate in training to develop and promote the organization's future leaders.

第2部 ユニバーシティサークルにおけるジュドソン 1906—2006 卓越の一世紀

「私たちはここで家族のようです。いい時もそうでないときも、そのことを分かち合っています」

ジュドソンメナーの屋上から

From the rooftop of Judson Manor.

6. Leading with Compassion and Vision

(1) In many cases the residents of Judson were themselves leaders—civic leaders, business leaders, education leaders, volunteer leaders, cultural leaders. Good leadership is something they value and something they receive at Judson.

"We offer options for smart living," says President and CEO, Cynthia Dunn.

Judson's location in University Circle has always appealed to those who are and have been engaged civically and culturally. Its residents are comfortable living in a diverse, urban environment.

As people have sought to take charge of their aging process, Judson has been there to give them tools—community outreach, wellness education, home health care, education and enrichment, socialization, volunteer opportunities and more.

"Judson is not a walled community. Its boundaries are permeable," she says.

Ms. Dunn has done it all at Judson. She began in 1978 as a resident advocate, helping people get settled. Very early on she bonded with the residents who supported her when her husband died and she was left alone to care for their three small children. "You don't live for 80 years without experiencing some loss. I learned early on that aging is a life process and the choices we make determine how we live."

While she loved the resident contact, Ms. Dunn has

第2部 ユニバーシティサークルにおけるジュドソン 1906—2006 卓越の一世紀

6 共感とビジョンをもって先頭に立つ

(1) 多くの場合ジュドソンのレジデントは自らリーダーである。市民リーダーであり、ビジネスリーダーであり、教育リーダーであり、ボランティアリーダーであり、文化的リーダーである。

よい意味のリーダーシップはレジデントが大切にしているものであり、またジュドソンで獲得するものでもある。

「私たちはスマートリビングのために色々なプログラムを提供できます」と会長兼CEO（最高経営責任者）のシンシア・ダンは言う。

ユニバーシティサークルにジュドソンがあること（ロケーション）は市民生活においてまた文化的意味において活動的であった人々をひきつけてきた。

レジデントは多様な、都市的な環境で快適に生活してきた人たちである。その人たちが自ら齢をとっていくプロセスに適切に対応できるよう求めているので、ジュドソンはそのための方法　―コミュニティとのつながり、健康教育、ホームヘルスケア、教育と豊かさ、社会とのつながり、ボランティア活動をする機会その他―　を提供してきた。

「ジュドソンは、壁に囲まれたコミュニティではありません。社会との境界線はお互いに浸透し合っています」と彼女は言う。

ダン会長はそれらすべてをジュドソンで実現することにかかわってきた。

彼女は1978年からレジデントの代弁者として、人々がジュドソンで安住の場を見つけるための支援をする仕事を行って来た。

早い時期に彼女の夫が亡くなり、3人の小さな子供たちの面倒を1人でみなければならなくなったとき以来、彼女を支えてくれたレジデントの人たちと彼女は深いつながりで結ばれてきた。

「人は80歳まで生きれば必ずいくらかのロスは生じます。私は早い

found the many facets of running Judson energize her professionally and personally. "I love forming strategies for successful leadership and for positioning us on the cutting edge of services and programs," she says.

(2) Judson has seen incredible growth while remaining true to its mission. As a result it has been able to attract business and community leaders at the peak of their careers to work or to serve on the board.

"I do enjoy the enthusiasm and energy Cyndy brings to issues," says Ann E. Zellmer, associate counsel at the Cleveland Clinic Foundation and chairman of the board of directors at Judson.

"It's a working board of dedicated people who want to add to the aging process. It's a roll-up-your-sleeves kind of experience. With a top-notch management team in place there's a real spirit of collaboration," she says.

"We're able to see a vibrant aging process brought to life and that's really something. You can't be around Cyndy Dunn and Sara Peckham without sharing their enjoyment and enthusiasm for people of all ages," she says.

John P. Schneider, senior vice president at National City Bank, and chairman of Judson Foundation, agrees.

"The way the board is structured provides us with a

時期から、齢を重ねていくことは人生のプロセスであり、私たち自らの選択によりいかに生きるかを決定するのだということを学びました」

彼女はレジデントとのつながりを大切にしているが、同時に彼女はジュドソンの経営に携わっていることに伴う様々な面が職業人としてもまた個人的にも彼女を元気づけることを発見した。

「私はリーダーシップが成功するように、またサービスとプログラムをよりよくしていくために、どのような立ち位置に立てばよいのかについての戦略を立てることが好きです」と彼女は言う。

(2) ジュドソンはその使命に忠実であった間に信じ難く成長した。結果としてジュドソンはビジネスリーダーやコミュニティリーダーをそのキャリアのピークにおいて惹きつけ、働きあるいは理事会での奉仕という協力を得ることができた。

クリーブランドクリニック財団の法律顧問でジュドソン理事会の長であるアン・E・ゼルマーは「私はシンシア・ダンが重要課題に注ぐ熱意とエネルギーを楽しんでいます」という。

「それは人々が歳を重ねていくプロセスに対し良い貢献ができることを願って努力している献身的な人々による働く理事会です。それは袖をまくりあげるような経験です。所を得た少数のトップマネジメントチームにより真の精神的な協力関係が出来上がっています」

「私たちは人が人生において齢を重ねていく過程を活気に満ちて生きる姿を見ることができます。そしてそれは実際重要なことです。シンシア・ダン会長やサラ・ペッカム部長に接すると、すべての年齢の人々に対する彼女らの喜びや熱意を共有せざるを得ません」

ジョン・P・シュナイダーは、ナショナルシティバンクの上席副頭取でジュドソン財団の会長であるが、その意見に同意する。「理事会の構成が多くの相互作用をもたらし、積極的な考えと共感に満

great deal of interaction, leading us toward forward thinking and compassionate leadership," he says.

第2部 ユニバーシティサークルにおけるジュドソン 1906—2006 卓越の一世紀

ちたリーダーシップをとるよう我々を導いてくれる」と彼はいう。

広域クリーブランドの市民のトップリーダーたちは、ジュドソンの「スマートリビング」のメッセージを信じ支援している。これらの人々はジュドソン100周年記念キャンペーンの成功のために中心的役割を果たした。
Greater Cleveland's top civic leaders believe in and support Judson's smart living message. These individuals were key to the success of Judson's Centennial Campaign.

7. Creating a Legacy

There's a distinct difference in working with a not-for-profit. "We have an opportunity to give back to the community through our programs and services that retain and attract older adults to the Greater Cleveland community," says Ms. Dunn.

Helping that effort along is the Judson Foundation. In 2002, Judson reorganized, creating the foundation as a separate, incorporated 501 (c) 3, under the parent company, Judson Services, Inc.

This new structure better reflects the significance of fund raising in helping the overall organization achieve its strategic goals. The Foundation also offers an opportunity for expanding board leadership and expertise specific to fund raising.

With programs in place for planned giving and the successful completion of the Centennial Capital Campaign, the Judson Foundation is poised to fill needs and gaps in services and facilities.

"As a not-for-profit, we continue to offer unique programs and services thanks to the generous support of foundations, donors and friends," notes Carol Markey, Vice President of Judson Foundation. "We wouldn't be who we are today without them."

第2部 ユニバーシティサークルにおけるジュドソン 1906—2006 卓越の一世紀

7 次代に残すべきもの

　非営利事業で働くことは他の事業で働くことと大きな違いがある。「広域クリーブランドのコミュニティに高齢の大人を留め、惹きつけるための私たちのプログラムやサービスは、コミュニティに対してお返しする役割を担っているのです」とシンシア・ダン会長は言う。

　その努力を共同して行うのはジュドソン財団である。2002年にジュドソンは組織を編成しなおし、ジュドソンサービス会社という親組織の下に、同じく非営利の別法人としてジュドソン財団を作った。この新しい枠組みは、全体組織がその戦略的目標を達成するために役立てるための募金活動の重要性を反映している。

　この財団は特に募金に向けた理事会のリーダーシップと専門知識を深めるための機会を提供してくれる。

　ジュドソン財団は、計画通り組織へ寄付が集まり、百年祭の募金活動を成功裏に終了できるよう適切な計画を立てることにより、組織のためにサービス・施設設備のニーズと現実とのギャップを埋めるためのバランスをとる立場に立っている。

　ジュドソン財団の副会長キャロル・マーケイは、「財団や寄付者や友人の寛大な支援のおかげで、非営利法人としてジュドソンは独自のプログラムやサービスを提供し続けています。彼らがいなければ私たちは現在のような姿でいることはできなかったでしょう」と付け加える。

8. Building on Success

"People are living longer, but we're shrinking the span of disability," says Ms. Dunn. "We have so much information regarding options for aging successfully. We know social engagement, and physical and mental 'exercise' are key elements. As an organization, we are committed to collaborating with partners who can help bring options and programs to those who choose to live in their homes as well as those who live in a Judson community," she says.

Judson stands for stability in this age of acquisitions and mergers. It's a testament to its leadership and governance over the years. "We want to be here for another 100 years," says Ms. Dunn.

"We're a disciplined, nimble organization, able to navigate the challenges, see future needs and take action."

Judson is expanding its geographic reach east with the introduction of South Franklin Circle. This sprawling 80-acre campus will provide a wide range of cottages, garden and town homes in the spectacular Chagrin Valley.

After years of study, the project is now underway. While the campus will cater primarily to independent living, it will also offer assisted living and access to the Bruening Health Center.

Ms. Dunn sees Judson as a three-legged stool with its supports being the University Circle campus, eastern campus and the community outreach services. "These give us a breadth of options that keep us viable and stable."

Over the next horizon Ms. Dunn sees building on and broadening the membership program, in addition to another

第2部 ユニバーシティサークルにおけるジュドソン 1906—2006 卓越の一世紀

8 建設計画の成功の上に

「人々は以前より長生きするようになっていますが、私たちは、人々が障害を持って生きる時間を短くすることに成功しています」とシンシア・ダン会長は言う。

「私たちは上手に歳をとるために必要な選択肢について大変多くの情報を持っています。私たちは社会契約や身体的精神的運動が鍵となる要素であることを知っています。組織として私たちは、ジュドソンコミュニティで生活する人々のためと同様に、自宅で生活することを選んだ人々に対しても適切な選択肢とプログラムを用意するための手助けをすることができる人々と協力することを約束しています」

　ジュドソンは現在のように組織の買収や合併が頻繁に行われる時代に、確固として独立を保っている。それは長年にわたるジュドソンのリーダーシップとガバナンスが適切であった証明である。
「私たちは、次の100年もここに存在したい」
「私たちは、規律ある敏捷な組織であり、挑戦に対して対応し、未来のニーズを見て行動を起こします」とダン会長は言う。
　ジュドソンはサウスフランクリンサークル（という新しい施設）の建設を進めており、地理的範囲を東に拡大しようとしている。
　そこでは不規則に広がった80エーカーの敷地内に、壮観なチャグリンの谷にある広くちらばった田舎風の小家屋、庭園、別邸を提供することになる。
　何年も研究したのち、このプロジェクトは今進行中である。
　最初は自立のレジデント向けの施設が作られるが、その後要支援のレジデント向け施設も用意され、そこから（ジュドソンパークの）ブリューニングヘルスセンターへも行けるように予定されている。

Part Two: Judson at University Circle 1906–2006 A Century of Excellence

residential campus in University Circle.

"From fairy humble beginnings Judson continues what I think is its mission established 100 years ago—to serve the older population and respect the aging process," says Mr. Schneider.

"We've been entrusted with a precious package. I feel humbled to be part of this mission-driven organization. During my watch, my duty is to keep it in good health and moving forward," says Ms. Dunn.

シンシア・H・ダン ジュドソン会長兼最高経営責任者
Cynthia H.Dunn, Judson President & CEO.

第2部 ユニバーシティサークルにおけるジュドソン 1906—2006 卓越の一世紀

　ダン会長はジュドソンをユニバーシティサークルにある施設と、サウスフランクリンサークルという東キャンパス及び近隣のコミュニティへのサービスという3つの柱を持つ3本脚の腰掛とみている。「これらは私たちに永続と安定をもたらしてくれる広い選択肢を与えてくれます」
　ユニバーシティサークルにあるもう一つの居住キャンパスに加え、ダン会長は次の地平線の向こうにメンバーシッププログラムを立ち上げ拡げていくことを思い描いている。

「かなりみすぼらしかった当初から、ジュドソンは私が考えるには、年長者に奉仕し、齢を重ねる過程を大切にするという100年前に確立された使命のために働き続けています」とシュナイダー氏は言う。
「私たちは貴重な包みを任せられているといってよいでしょう。私は使命に突き動かされた組織に加わっていることを謙虚に誇りに思っています。私が見ている間は、私の義務はジュドソンを健全な組織として、前進させることです」とダン会長は言う。

建設中の新施設、サウス・フランクリン・サークルの完成予想図
An Elevation for South Franklin Circle, a new Judson campus.

Part Two: Judson at University Circle 1906–2006 A Century of Excellence

9. Epilogue

Did those well-meaning women of the Euclid Avenue Baptist Church know what they started in 1906?
Whether or not they could see 100 years into the future, they set in motion a mission, indeed an example for smart living that has withstood the test of time. Judson is proud of its care, its residents, its people, its vision and its tradition.

全盛時代のユークリッド通り
Euclid Avenue in its heyday.

第2部 ユニバーシティサークルにおけるジュドソン 1906—2006 卓越の一世紀

9 エピローグ

　ユークリッド通りバプティスト教会の善意の婦人たちは1906年に何を始めたのか十分理解していただろうか。100年後を見通すことができたかどうかにかかわりなく、100年の「時」の試練に耐えたスマートリビングのための見本ともいうべき使命の働きを始めたのである。ジュドソンは、ジュドソンのケア、ジュドソンのレジデント、ジュドソンの人々、ビジョン、伝統を誇りにしている。

北オハイオバプティストホームは1939年、
伝説的なビックネルマンションに移って来た。
The Baptist Home of Northern Ohio relocated
to the legendary Bicknell Mansion in 1939.

第3部

カウンシル・オブ・インターナショナル・プログラムズ USA
（CIPUSA）

Part Three

Council of International Programs USA (CIPUSA)

Part Three: Council of International Programs USA (CIPUSA)

1. The interview to Dr. Ollendorff tells us about the birth of CIP

(1) I studied at Judson as an intern by the invitation of CIP as I wrote. I want to write more about CIP. I have a good source of material to know how CIP was born.

It is a copy of a booklet of an interview by the Bureau of Educational and Cultural Affairs of the Department of State the title of which is "A Brief History of the Council of International Programs 1954–1976 (By Henry B. Ollendorff in his own words)". Dr. Ollendorff is the founder of CIP.
It was distributed to each of the participants of the 27th Council of International Fellowship (CIF) Conference in Cleveland held in 2007. I participated in the conference and I got it.

The introduction on the first page of the booklet is as follows:

In the fall of 1972, the Bureau of Educational and Cultural Affairs of the Department of State (CU), began to organize its files into an historical archive, to write or have written under contract a history and to conduct a series of taped interviews with persons in and out of Government who had long been associated with the Department's programs of educational and cultural relations. This interview with Henry B. Ollendorff is one of many such and the first to be transcribed and edited.
It should be noted that the Bureau of Educational and Cultural Affairs (CU) and the U.S. Information Agency (USIA) were amalgamated to form the U.S. International Communication

第3部 カウンシル・オブ・インターナショナル・プログラムズUSA（CIPUSA）

1 オレンドルフ博士へのインタビューが伝えるCIP誕生の物語

(1) 前述したように私はCIPの招きによりジュドソンで研修することとなった。ここでCIPについてさらに述べてみたい。CIPの誕生について知るにはよい資料がある。

　それは『カウンシル・オブ・インターナショナル・プログラムズの簡潔な歴史1954－1976（ヘンリー・B・オレンドルフが自ら語る）』というタイトルのアメリカ国務省教育文化局によるインタビューの小冊子のコピーである。ヘンリー・B・オレンドルフ博士はCIPの創設者である。

　その冊子は2007年にクリーブランドで開かれたカウンシル・オブ・インターナショナル・フェロウシップ（CIF）の第27回大会の参加者に配布されたものであり、参加した私はそこで手に入れた。

　その冊子の最初のページには前置きとして次のように書かれている。

　1972年秋、米国国務省の教育文化局は、所蔵ファイルを歴史公文書館に系統立てて整理し、契約によって歴史を記録し、政府関係者であると否とを問わず国務省の教育文化関係の計画プログラムに長期に関わった人々についてのインタビューをテープ化してシリーズにまとめることを始めた。

　ヘンリー・B・オレンドルフへのこのインタビューは、このような多くのインタビューのひとつであり、最初にテープをおこして編集されたものである。

　教育文化局と広報・文化交流庁は、国際交流庁を作るため1978年4月1日にカーター大統領の1977年組織変更計画No.2により合併したことは特記されるべきである。※

Part Three: Council of International Programs USA (CIPUSA)

Agency on April 1, in 1978 under President Carter's Reorganization Plan No. 2 of 1977.(*)

(*)
The International Communication Agency which was established April 1, 1978, by authority of Reorganization Plan No. 2 of 1977, was redesignated as the United States Information Agency by section 303(a) of the United States Information Agency Authorization Act, Fiscal Years 1982 and 1983 (96 Stat. 291).
(Source: U.S. Government Manual 1983/84)
Under Foreign Affairs Restructuring and Reform Act of 1998, USIA was integrated with the Department of State as of October 1, 1999.

(2) I write about the birth of CIP by the help of this interview as a source.
Dr. Henry B. Ollendorff was born in Germany and worked as a labor lawyer. During the beginning of Hitler days, he spent about 13 months in prison.
He came to America with his wife Martha in 1938. Instead of starting to study American law all over again he went into social work. He studied at what was then Columbia University Graduate School of Social Work.
In 1940 he came to Cleveland. He got a job of a settlement house in the black ghetto area in Cleveland. It was the only job he could get. He started as a worker and five years later became the executor of the association of several settlement houses in Cleveland.

第3部 カウンシル・オブ・インターナショナル・プログラムズ USA（CIPUSA）

※ 1977年の組織変更計画 No.2 により 1978年4月1日に設置された国際交流庁は 1982・1983 会計年度の広報・文化交流庁授権法 303条(a) により広報・文化交流庁と呼ばれることとなった。（法令集 96巻 291 頁）。（出所：米国政府マニュアル 1983/84))

その後、1998年外務組織再編改革法により広報・文化交流庁は1999年10月1日をもって国務省に統合された。

(2) 私はこのインタビューをもとに CIP 誕生の物語を書く。

ヘンリー・B・オレンドルフ博士はドイツで生まれ、労働関係の法律家として働いた。ヒットラー時代の初めに、13か月間牢獄で過ごした。

彼は妻マルタとともに1938年にアメリカにやって来た。

アメリカの法律を隅々まで勉強することを始める代わりに、ソーシャルワークの分野に入った。今日コロンビア大学のソーシャルワーク大学院と呼ばれているところで勉強した。

1940年に彼はクリーブランドにやって来た。そしてクリーブランドの黒人ゲットー（貧しい人の街）地区のセツルメントハウスの仕事に就いた。それが彼の得ることのできた唯一の仕事だった。はじめはワーカーとして働き、5年後にはクリーブランドのいくつかのセツルメントハウスの連合体の責任者となった。

Part Three: Council of International Programs USA (CIPUSA)

In 1954, he received a letter from the Department of State, with which he had had no dealings whatsoever. It was a letter to invite him to go to Germany for five months to teach as one of the instructors in a training school which US military government originally set up outside of Frankfurt for German Jewish leaders.
(After the Second World War, Germany was occupied by America, U.K., France and Soviet Union.)
He accepted the invitation.

He spent five months in 1954 as a "U.S. Specialist" in Germany and find out about social work and youth work as it was practiced at that time. But most of the time he taught together with one or two other Americans this seminar.

The people whom he taught were volunteer youth leaders of the newer generation. A few of them were professional social workers. One or two had been in the States already on an exchange program in 1954.
The impressions he got there caused him, when he went back to Cleveland to his regular social work job again, to get a group of leading Cleveland citizens together for a sponsoring committee to invite to Cleveland for a summer program some of the young German volunteer youth leaders whom he met in Germany.

He endeavored to realize this idea. He went back to old contacts. One of his friends was a Foreign Service Officer (at that time Director of the Office of Public Affairs in the Bureau of German and Austrian Affairs). With his cooperation the Fulbright Commission in Germany gave 15 travel grants for

第3部 カウンシル・オブ・インターナショナル・プログラムズUSA（CIPUSA）

1954年に彼はそれまで何のつながりもなかった国務省から1通の手紙をもらった。それはドイツ占領のアメリカ軍政府がドイツのユダヤ人指導者のためにフランクフルト近郊にもともと設置していた訓練学校でインストラクターの1人として教えるために5か月間ドイツへ行くよう招待するというものだった（第2次大戦後ドイツは米英仏ソ連に占領されていた）。彼はその申し出を受諾した。

彼は1954年にアメリカ人専門家としてドイツで5か月間を過ごし、当時ソーシャルワークとユースワークがどのように行われているかを学んだ。しかし大半の時間は1〜2名の他のアメリカ人とこのセミナーで教えながら過ごした。

彼が教えたのは新世代のボランティアユースリーダーだった。そのうち何名かはプロのソーシャルワーカーであった。1人か2人は1954年に交換プログラムですでにアメリカへ行ってきた人だった。

そしてそこで得た印象から彼がクリーブランドへ帰って再びいつものソーシャルワークの仕事に戻ったとき、指導的なクリーブランドの市民グループに働きかけて、ドイツで彼が会った若いドイツのボランティアユースリーダーたちの中から何人かを夏のプログラムのためにクリーブランドへ招くためのスポンサーとなる委員会を作りたいという考えが浮かんだ。

彼はこのアイディアの実現のために努力した。彼は古くからの人とのつながりに立ち返った。彼の友人の1人は外交官（当時ドイツ・オーストリア局の公務部の部長）であった。この人の協力により、ドイツのフルブライト委員会がクリーブランドでの実践的プログラムへのドイツからの参加者のために15名分の旅費助成金を出してくれた。

このプロジェクトのために守るべき3項目が定められた。参加者の選考には必ず自分たちが参加すること。短期間（4か月）とすべきであり、プログラムの大半は実践的な実地の現場（フィールド）

the German participants in a practical experience program in Cleveland.

To realize this project 3 points were decided to keep.
They have to participate in the selections of the participants.
It should be a short-term thing (four months) and most of it should be a practical field experience.
The participants should live not in a dormitory or in a hotel but with American families.
In addition to these 3 points, the interview to select participants should be done in English.

Moreover by the help of an old school friend of his who had become the Deputy in the Bundestag (the Federal Parliament of Germany), the Ministry of Youth and Sports in Germany sent ten participants to the program.
So they had 25 German participants, youth leaders, a few social workers for four months in Cleveland from the end of May until the end of August in 1956. They were housed with host families.

In Cleveland they had formed a citizens sponsoring committee composed of volunteers.
They got a committee together of board members of social agencies such as the Girl Scouts, YMCA and so on.
They had two original grants from the Cleveland Foundation and from the Cleveland Rotary Club.
They recruited volunteer host families and the participants stayed for two weeks with one family. So they had five different families in ten weeks.
They arranged through and with people at the School of Social

第3部 カウンシル・オブ・インターナショナル・プログラムズ USA（CIPUSA）

体験であるべきだということ。参加者は寮やホテルではなくアメリカ人の家庭に宿泊すべきであること。
　これら3点に加え、参加者の選考のための面接は英語で行うべきことが加えられた。
　その上彼の昔の級友でドイツ連邦議会の議員になっていた人の助けを得て、ドイツの青年・スポーツ省が10名を送り込んできた。
　そのため25名のユースリーダー・ソーシャルワーカーからなるドイツ人が、1956年の5月の終わりから8月の終わりまでの4か月間クリーブランドでのプログラムに参加した。彼らはホストファミリー宅に宿泊した。

　クリーブランドではボランティアの市民による支援のための委員会が結成された。ガールスカウトやYMCA等の社会組織の役員とともに委員会が作られた。クリーブランド財団やクリーブランドロータリークラブが最初から助成金を出してくれた。人々はボランティアのホストファミリーを募り、参加者は1家族のところに2週間滞在した。そして10週間に5軒のホストファミリー宅に滞在した。
　人々は参加者たちがアメリカについて理解を深めるための5〜6週間の入門プログラムをケース・ウエスタンリザーブ大学のソーシャルワーク校の人々と共に後援するための準備をした。
　そして参加者たちは10週間のフィールドワークに参加した。彼らは働かねばならなかった。ぶらぶら歩きをしたり、傍観していることは許されなかった。参加者全員がユースキャンプと子供キャンプの指導員の役を割り当てられた。
　すべてが終了したとき、関係者全員で評価が行われた。

　最初の計画では、このプログラムは1956年だけのものであった。しかし彼らは言った。
　「これはやめてはいけない。次も行うべきだ。続けるべきだ。そしてドイツに限定してはならない。多国間の事業にしなければならない」

Part Three: Council of International Programs USA (CIPUSA)

Work at the Case Western Reserve University for the sponsorship with them for five- six weeks of introductory programs to acquaint the participants with the United States.
And then they went to field work for ten weeks. They should work, and not just hang around and observe.
All of them were assigned to youth and children's camps as camp counselors.
When it was all over, it was evaluated by everybody concerned.

In the first plan the program was only for 1956. But they said "Now, don't stop, do it again, continue it, but don't limit it to Germany, make it a multinational affair."

This is the story of the birth of CIP which the interview to Dr. Ollendorff tells us.

In the following pages, I write about the development of CIP excerpting from the home pages of the organizations concerned.

第3部 カウンシル・オブ・インターナショナル・プログラムズ USA（CIPUSA）

　これがオレンドルフ博士へのインタビューが語るCIP誕生の物語である。

　次にCIPのその後の発展について関係組織のホームページからの引用により示すことにしたい。

Part Three: Council of International Programs USA (CIPUSA)

2. The wish of Dr. Ollendorff and CIPUSA

More than 50 years have passed since then.
The wish of Dr. Ollendorff is written as follows in the home page of CIF International:
"Dr. Ollendorff had a vision to create an international program where youth leaders and social workers from many countries could get together with the goal that the horrors of Second World War would never happen again." (Home Page of CIF International, 18 June 2009)

The program has grown up as a big multinational affair.
The program has been carried on by the Council of International Programs USA. The home page of it tells us as follows:
"The Council of International Programs USA is committed to promoting international understanding through professional development and cross-cultural exchange.
Since the beginning, CIPUSA has brought over 10,000 international professionals from 147 countries to the U.S. for practical training in an array of disciplines.
We believe that tolerance and understanding among people are built through cultural exchange experiences and we work hard to create the best experiences possible for each of our participants.
CIPUSA conducts training programs throughout the Unite States. CIPUSA's national office is located in Cleveland, Ohio. It has eight affiliate offices nationwide." (Home Page of CIPUSA, 7 November 2008)

第3部 カウンシル・オブ・インターナショナル・プログラムズ USA（CIPUSA）

2 オレンドルフ博士の願いと CIPUSA

　以来50年以上が経過した。
　オレンドルフ博士の願いについてCIFインターナショナルのホームページには次のように書かれている。
「オレンドルフ博士は多くの国々のユースリーダーやソーシャルワーカーが第2次大戦の恐怖を2度と経験することのない世界を作るために集いあう国際的プログラムを作ろうというヴィジョンを持っていた」（CIFインターナショナルのホームページ2009.6.18）

　CIPのプログラムは大きな多国間の事業に発展した。この事業はカウンシル・オブ・インターナショナル・プログラムズUSAによって今日まで担われてきている。そのホームページは次のように伝えている。

「カウンシル・オブ・インターナショナル・プログラムズUSAは職業的能力向上と異文化交流を通して国際理解を深めるために努めている。活動を始めて以来CIPUSAは規律ある実践的トレーニングのために147か国から10,000人以上の国際的職業人をアメリカへ招待してきた。
　私たちは人々の間の寛容と理解は異文化交流を通して得られることを信じており、また私たちは参加者1人ひとりが可能な最高の経験ができるよう努めている。CIPUSAはアメリカの全国規模でトレーニングプログラムを実施している。CIPUSAのナショナルオフィスはオハイオ州クリーブランドに置かれている。また全国に8つの支部がある」（CIPUSAのホームページ2008.11.7）

Part Three: Council of International Programs USA (CIPUSA)

3. Council of International Fellowship (CIF)

CIF
The past participants of CIP program made an organization by the name of the Council of International Fellowship (CIF).
"The Council of International Fellowship (CIF) is a private, voluntary, non-profit, politically and religiously independent organization founded in 1960 following up the Cleveland International Program in the USA-later on Council of International Programs (CIP) and CIPUSA.
In 1960, alumni of CIP, keen to share this spirit of fellowship, founded CIF. Since then 31 countries throughout Africa, Asia, Europe, Middle East, North and South America and Oceania have established National Branches. Twenty two of them also run programs with similar aims to that first CIP. The General Assembly and the Board of Directors which meet biannually during an international conference co-organized and hosted by one of the National Branches." (Home Page of CIF International, 18 June 2009)

CIF-Japan
"Since 1962 around 130 Japanese, engaging in social work or research in social welfare, have participated to the CIPUSA Program or the CIF Exchange Programs. After returning home they have contributed with their experience in the various professional fields and also strived for improving their

3 カウンシル・オブ・インターナショナル・フェロウシップ（CIF）

CIF

　過去のCIP研修参加者がカウンシル・オブ・インターナショナル・フェロウシップという名の組織を創っている。

「カウンシル・オブ・インターナショナル・フェロウシップ（CIF）はアメリカのクリーブランド・インターナショナル・プログラム—後にカウンシル・オブ・インターナショナル・プログラムズ（CIP）—とCIPUSAの事業をさらに推し進めるべく1960年に私的ボランタリーの非営利・政治的宗教的に中立の組織として創設された。

　1960年に友愛の精神を共有することに敏感なCIP卒業生がCIFを創設した。それ以来、アフリカ・アジア・ヨーロッパ・中東・南北アメリカ・オセアニアをカバーする31カ国がナショナルブランチ（各国の支部）を立ち上げた。それらのうち22か国が初期のCIPと同様の目的をもってプログラムを実施している。2年に1度国際会議の間に開かれる総会と理事会は各国の支部の1つが共同で組織し、主催国をつとめる。」（CIFインターナショナルのホームページ2009.6.18）

CIFジャパン

「1962年以来今日まで、わが国から130名余りの社会福祉従事者、研究者が米国のCIP研修プログラムはじめ各国交流研修に参加し、帰国後、それぞれの専門の職域において貢献し、又自ら専門性の向上に努めてまいりました。

　その後1986年、帰国者有志によりCIFジャパンを結成し、CIF国

Part Three: Council of International Programs USA (CIPUSA)

proficiency.

In 1986 some of these CIPUSA or CIF alumni members voluntarily organized CIF Japan, that was admitted to join CIF International as a National Branch. Presently, CIF Japan is supporting those applicants who desire to participate in CIPUSA or CIF Exchange Programs.

Further it is expected CIF Japan will set up and start Exchange Program in Japan near future". (Home Page of CIF-Japan, 24 June 2009)

We can get more information about CIP and CIF in the following home pages.

1. Council of International Programs USA (CIPUSA)
　　　　　　　　　　　　http://www.cipusa.org/
2. CIF International　　　http://www.cifinternational.com/
3. CIF-Japan　　　　　　http://cif-japan.papnet.jp/
4. CIF Aotearoa/New Zealand http://www.cif.org.nz/
5. CIF Australia　　　　　http://www.cifaustralia.org/
6. CIF Austria　　　　　　http://www.cifaustria.at/
7. CIF Estonia　　　　　　http://www.cifestonia.ee/
8. CIF Finland　　　　　　http://www.ciffinland.org/
9. CIF France　　　　　　http://www.cif-france.org/
10. CIF Germany　　　　http://www.cif-germany.de/
11. CIF Hellas /Greece　　http://www.cifhellas.org/
12. CIF Italy　　　　　　　http://www.cifitalia.it/
13. CIF Norway　　　　　http://cifnorway.org/
14. CIF Scotland　　　　　http://www.cifscotland.org.uk/
15. CIF Sweden　　　　　http://www.cif-sweden.org/

第3部 カウンシル・オブ・インターナショナル・プログラムズ USA（CIPUSA）

際グループのメンバーとなりました。
　現在、米国及び各国の研修プログラム応募者の参加支援事業を実施しています。さらに近い将来、わが国での交流研修プログラムの開催、実施が期待されています」（CIFジャパンのホームページ2009.6.24）

　CIPとCIFのより詳しい情報は以下のホームページで得ることができる。

1. Council of International Programs USA (CIPUSA)
　　　　　　　　　　　　http://www.cipusa.org/
2. CIF International　　　http://www.cifinternational.com/
3. CIF-Japan　　　　　　http://cif-japan.papnet.jp/
4. CIF Aotearoa/Newzealand http://www.cif.org.nz/
5. CIF Australia　　　　　http://www.cifaustralia.org/
6. CIF Austria　　　　　　http://www.cifaustria.at/
7. CIF Estonia　　　　　　http://www.cifestonia.ee/
8. CIF Finland　　　　　　http://www.ciffinland.org/
9. CIF France　　　　　　http://www.cif-france.org/
10. CIF Germany　　　　　http://www.cif-germany.de/
11. CIF Hellas/Greece　　　http://www.cifhellas.org/
12. CIF Italy　　　　　　　http://www.cifitalia.it/
13. CIF Norway　　　　　　http://cifnorway.org/
14. CIF Scotland　　　　　http:www.cifscotland.org.uk/
15. CIF Sweden　　　　　　http://www.cif-sweden.org/

Source books and Reference material

Part One
1 Home page of the Eden Alternative
2 Japanese National Committee of the International Council on Social Welfare, "Project for training abroad: International Training Program (CIP) for those engaged in social welfare in 1996," (pamphlet in Japanese)
3 Home page of CIPUSA
4 Tanaka Hideo (ed.), "Dictionary of Anglo-American Law" (University of Tokyo Press, 1991)
5 Kurokawa Yukiko, "Reminiscence—Psychological Therapy for the Elderly" (in Japanese) (Seishin Shobo, 2005)

Part Two
Judson Retirement Community, "Judson at University Circle 1906–2006 A Century of Excellence" (Judson Retirement Community, 2006)

Part Three
1 The Bureau of Educational and Cultural Affairs of the Department of State, "A Brief History of the Council of International Programs 1954–1976 (By Henry B. Ollendorff in his own words)" (The Bureau of Educational and Cultural Affairs of the Department of State)
2 U.S. Government Manual 1983/84
3 Home page of CIF International
4 Home page of CIPUSA
5 Home page of CIF-Japan

出典・引用参考文献

第 1 章
1 エデン・オールターナティブ ホームページ
2 国際社会福祉協議会日本国委員会『海外研修派遣事業 社会福祉従事者のための国際研修プログラム (CIP) 参加候補者募集要綱（1996年派遣）』（パンフレット）
3 CIPUSA ホームページ
4 田中英夫（編集代表）『英米法辞典』［東京大学出版会、1991 年］
5 黒川由紀子『回想法―高齢者の心理療法』［誠信書房、2005 年］

第 2 章
ジュドソン・リタイアメント・コミュニティ『ユニバーシティサークルにおけるジュドソン 1906-2006 卓越の一世紀』［ジュドソン・リタイアメント・コミュニティ、2006 年］

第 3 章
1 米国国務省教育文化局『カウンシル・オブ・インターナショナル・プログラムズの簡潔な歴史 1954-1976（ヘンリー・B・オレンドルフが自ら語る）』［米国国務省教育文化局］
2 米国政府マニュアル 1983/84
3 CIF インターナショナル ホームページ
4 CIPUSA ホームページ
5 CIF ジャパン ホームページ

Postscript

Now is the era when the life term after retirement is getting longer and longer.
A very important theme now is how we should live in the latter half of our lives.
Thirteen years ago I had an experience to study as an intern at Judson Retirement Community in America which was a facility for the elderly. According to the principles of Judson, the key components to live lives to the fullest in the latter half of lives are physical activity, encouraging intellectual stimulation and close contact with the community. There I watched the active lives of the residents, the highly motivated management and staff, and the close contacts of the residents with people in the neighboring communities. It showed what should be wished for in the facilities for the elderly.
 I am very pleased to be able to write about Judson Retirement Community in the centennial publication of Judson.

Council of International Programs USA (CIPUSA) which invited me to the United States to study as an intern has brought more than 10,000 international professionals from 147 countries to the United States. It promotes international understanding through professional development and cross-cultural exchange. I got the chance to write about CIPUSA in Part Three of this book.

Some parts of this book are written by me. The other parts are from other publications, summary or excerpt of other material. I wrote Part One both in English and Japanese. In Part Two I

あとがき

　人々の寿命が延び、退職後の生活がますます長くなる時代にあって、後半生をいかに生きるかが時代の大きなテーマとなっている。
　私は13年前、アメリカの高齢者施設ジュドソン・リタイアメント・コミュニティで研修し学ぶ機会があった。そこでは人生の後半を充実して生きるために、健康を支える身体運動を行うこと、知的刺激を高めること、社会と密接に関わることの3つを重要な要素として利用者の支援を行っていた。そこで利用者の活発な生活、働く人々の意欲的な姿、近隣の人々との積極的な関わり等、生き生きとした姿を目の辺りにし、高齢者施設のありかたに大きな示唆を得た。
　このたび高齢者施設ジュドソン・リタイアメント・コミュニティの100年記念誌の内容の紹介をすることができてとても嬉しい。

　私を研修にアメリカへ招いてくれたカウンシル・オブ・インターナショナル・プログラムズUSA (CIPUSA)という団体は、本文に書いたように現在まで50年以上にわたって世界147か国から10,000人以上の職業人をアメリカに招き、職業的能力向上と異文化交流を通じて国際理解を深める活動を行っている。この団体についても本書の第3部で紹介することができた。

　本書の内容には、他の出版物その他の資料の内容そのままの紹介や要約引用したもの及び編著者が書き下ろしたものがある。第1部は和文・英文とも編著者の梶村が書き下ろし、第2部は100年記念誌（英文）からの和訳を編著者が行ったもの、第3部では英文の要約・引用部分は編著者が和訳したが、その他は和文・英文双方がそろった文の引用以外は編著者が和文・英文ともに書き下ろしたものである。

　本書は多くの方々の協力を得て完成した。

translated the centennial publication of Judson into Japanese. In Part Three I translated the summarized and excerpted parts in English into Japanese and wrote the other part both in English and Japanese except in the case of excerpting the same sentences in English and Japanese.

This book was written by the help of the persons as follows:
Ms. Cynthia H. Dunn, President and CEO of Judson Retirement Community offered me the permission to use the centennial publication of Judson, other material and photos of Judson for this book. She also corrected some parts in this book.
Ms. Dorothy A. Faller, ex-CEO of CIPUSA corrected English expression in the book.
Ms. Lisa Purdy, the current CEO of CIPUSA and Mr. Takeuchi Kazutoshi, President of CIF-Japan offered me the permission of excerpting from the respective home pages for this book.
Professor Emeritus Kato Yuzo, former President of Yokohama City University gave me a lot of useful advice for this book.
Dr. Kinoshita Tsuyoshi, ex-professor of Hokkaido University, etc., former representative director of Japanese American Society for Legal Studies, currently attorney-at-law, gave me teachings about American law for this book.
Ms. Carol & Mr. John Battle, Ms. Carol & Mr. Al. Schupp and Ms. Georgia & Mr. Whitney Lloyd were the host families when I was an intern at Judson 13 years ago. I had so nice experiences at their homes. Ms. Carol & Mr. John Battle gave me advice about English expression and Mr. John got in touch with Judson for my book.
I would like to express my hearty thanks to all the persons

ジュドソン・リタイアメント・コミュニティの会長兼CEO Ms. Cynthia H. Dunnには100年記念誌の利用許可のほか、資料や写真の提供、内容の誤りの訂正等をしていただいた。CIPUSAの前CEO Ms. Dorothy A. Fallerには本書全体について編著者の英語表現に関し必要な修正をしていただいた。CIPUSAの現CEO Ms. Lisa PurdyとCIFジャパン会長竹内和利氏からは、それぞれCIPUSAとCIFジャパンのホームページからの引用許可をいただいた。

　編著者の学生時代からの先輩である横浜市立大学元学長の加藤祐三名誉教授には本書全体にわたって貴重なご助言をいただいた。学生時代からの先輩で、北海道大学等で教鞭をとられ、日米法学会代表理事等を歴任され、現在弁護士の木下毅氏（法学博士）にはアメリカ法を中心に貴重なご教示をいただいた。

　また、13年前のアメリカ研修中にホームステイ先のMs. Carol & Mr. John Battle、Ms. Carol & Mr. Al. Schupp、Ms. Georgia & Mr. Whitney Lloydにはアメリカ市民生活のすばらしい体験をさせていただいたが、中でもMs. CarolとMr. John Battleには英語表現に関し助言をいただき、またMr. Johnには本書作成の過程でジュドソンへの連絡等の労を取っていただいた。

　その他多くの方々のご支援をいただいたが、これらすべての方々に心からの感謝を申し述べたい。

　出版にさいして株式会社JPS出版局の高石左京氏にお世話になった。厚く御礼申し上げる。

2010年1月
編・著者　梶村慎吾

above.

Mr. Takaishi Sakyo of JPS Publishing worked hard to publish this book. I express my deep thanks to him.

In January, 2010
Editor: Kajimura Shingo

梶村慎吾
昭和14年生まれ 東京大学法学部卒業
22年間社会福祉法人賛育会において社会福祉事業に従事し、病院事務長、軽費老人ホーム・特別養護老人ホーム施設長、法人(本部)法務部長(業務五部長)等をつとめた。
また、東京都社会福祉協議会老人福祉部会経営検討委員会委員長、東京都社会福祉協議会福祉サービス第三者評価事業専門員(経営・福祉担当)、全国軽費老人ホーム協議会理事、町田市介護保険事業計画審議会部会委員、町田市介護認定審査会委員、(東京都包括補助事業)町田市痴呆性(認知症)高齢者グループホームあり方検討委員会委員長等をつとめた。
現在、医療法人社団温知会理事ほか医療法人、財団法人等役員をつとめている。
著作
編著 「社会福祉におけるコンプライアンス」[太陽出版、2007年] ほか
連絡先 Eメール:fukushiken591@tbt.t-com.ne.jp

Kajimura Shingo
Engaged in social welfare work for 22 years. (Now) Director of Onchikai Medical Corporation, etc.
Author (ed.): " Compliance in Social Welfare Service : New Edition" (Taiyo Publishing, 2007), etc.
E-mail: fukushiken591@tbt.t-com.ne.jp

人生を豊かに生きるために必要なものは何か
理想の高齢者施設を求めて
——ジュドソン・リタイアメント・コミュニティに学ぶ——
梶村慎吾 編・著

What do we need to live our lives with satisfaction?
To make ideal facilities for the elderly
——learning from Judson Retirement Community——
Edited by Kajimura Shingo

2010年2月15日 初版発行   日英対訳

発行者	高石 左京
発行所	JPS出版局
	編集室:神奈川県秦野市下大槻410-1-20-301 〒257-0004
	e-mail:jps@aqua.ocn.ne.jp FAX:0463-76-7195
装 幀	勝谷 高子(ウインバレー)
DTP	小島 展明
印刷・製本	株式会社 シナノパブリッシングプレス
発売元	太陽出版
	東京都文京区本郷4-1-14 〒113-0033
	TEL:03-3814-0471 FAX:03-3814-2366

©Kajimura Shingo, 2010 Printed in Japan. ISBN978-4-88469-629-0

── 好評発売中 ──
社会福祉におけるコンプライアンス

梶村慎吾　編・著
A5判上製　本文 304 頁
定価（本体 2800 円＋税）
太陽出版刊

激変する経営環境／優良組織をどの様に構築するか
社会福祉経営者・管理職・リーダー層必携の書
公益通報者保護法・改正介護保険法の施行、公益法人制度改革関連3法の制定。コンプライアンスを欠けば組織は根底から揺らぎかねない。社会福祉関係者はどう対応すべきかを詳述し、主な関連法令を網羅する。

....

Compliance in Social Welfare Service: New Edition
Book about Compliance in Social Welfare Service of Japan (in Japanese)

Edited and written by Kajimura Shingo
Taiyo Publishing